READY TO READ MORE

A Skills-Based Reader

Karen Blanchard

Christine Root

PEARSON

Longman

This series is dedicated to our students—past, present, and future.

Ready to Read More: A Skills-Based Reader

Pearson Education, 10 Bank Street, White Plains, NY 10606

Executive editor: Laura Le Dréan
Acquisitions editor: Lucille M. Kennedy
Development editor: Dana Klinek
Production editor: Diana P. George
Production coordinator: Melissa Leyva
Marketing manager: Timothy Benell
Senior manufacturing buyer: Nancy Flaggman
Photo research: Shana McGuire
Cover design: Pat Wosczyk
Cover image: © April/Getty Images
Text design: Pat Wosczyk
Text composition: Laserwords
Text font: 11.5/13 Minion
Text art: Jill Wood, pp. 31, 166, 167; Burmar Technical Services, pp. 34, 106, 145, 173
Photo and text credits: vi

Library of Congress Cataloging-in-Publication Data

Blanchard, Karen Lourie, 1951-
  Ready to read more / by Karen Blanchard and Christine Root.
    p. cm.
  ISBN 0-13-177649-5 (alk. paper)
  1. English language—Textbooks for foreign speakers. 2. Reading—Problems, exercises, etc. 3. Readers.
I. Root, Christine Baker, 1945– II. Title.

PE1128.B5867 2006
428.6'4—dc22

2005007813

ISBN: 0-13-177649-5

Printed in the United States of America
4 5 6 7 8 9 10—[BAH]—12 11 10 09 08 07

Contents

Scope and Sequence

CHAPTER	READING SKILLS	VOCABULARY SKILLS	LONG READINGS	GO BEYOND THE TEXT
1 **Think Before You Read**	Previewing and predicting	Word parts: Prefixes	*Reaching High and Living Long* *Living Past 100*	Making a list Making a poster
2 **Identify Main Ideas**	Identifying main ideas and topics	Word parts: Noun suffixes	*The Silk Road;* *Yo-Yo Ma and the Silk Road Project*	Designing a CD cover
3 **Use Vocabulary Strategies**	Using context to guess meaning	Vocabulary in context	*Big Talkers* *Koalas*	Completing a chart Preparing an oral report
4 **Understand Supporting Details**	Identifying supporting details	Vocabulary in context Word parts: Adjective suffixes Pronoun reference	*The Power of Advertising;* *International Marketing* *No Va*	Translating a foreign advertising slogan Planning and acting out a TV commercial
5 **Analyze the Text**	Recognizing patterns of organization	Word parts: Verb suffixes	*Race to the End of the Earth* *Lance Armstrong*	Writing a journal entry
6 **Make Inferences**	Making inferences	Compound words	*Fortune-Telling* *The Fortune Sellers*	Writing fortunes
7 **Distinguish Fact from Opinion**	Distinguishing fact from opinion	Collocations	*Seattle* *The Best Cities in the United States*	Taking a survey Using charts
8 **Understand the Author's Purpose and Tone**	Identifying purpose and tone	Connotation and denotation Verb + noun collocations Noun + verb collocations	*Why the Sea Is Salty* *Why Is the Ocean Salty?*	Discussing or creating a folktale

Credits

Introduction

Like its companion writing series, *Ready to Write*, the **Ready to Read** series comprises three task-based, skill-building textbooks for students of English. Also like its sister series, the reading series is skills-based and user-friendly, a series that both teachers and students will find easy to follow and use. **Ready to Read More**, the highest level book in the series, focuses on helping students refine and hone the reading skills required for efficient, confident, and independent academic and pleasure reading.

THE APPROACH

The books in the **Ready to Read** series are made up of task-based chapters, each of which has reading and vocabulary skill-building as its primary focus. For this series we started by choosing the reading and vocabulary skills we wanted to teach in each chapter and then selected readings for their value in helping students understand and practice those specific skills.

As a skill is presented, paintings, photographs, graphics, examples, and short texts, both prose and non-prose, are used to illustrate that skill and provide practice. Each chapter opens with a pictorial representation of a reading skill to give students a nonverbal reference point. The reading skill is then practiced throughout the text, recycled and reinforced in every subsequent chapter. The intrinsic difficulty of each individual skill dictates whether it is a skill that is recycled throughout the series or introduced and practiced only in books two and/or three. For example, foundational skills such as distinguishing main ideas from supporting details appear in all three books, while skills such as understanding an author's purpose and tone appear only in the later books.

In addition to demonstrating comprehension through standard exercises, students work with visual representations of readings by completing a chart, graph, table, or outline as they read. Graphic organizers of this sort help students look at and understand the basic structure of a reading and the interrelationships among ideas as well as anticipate and follow the author's intent.

Like the *Ready to Write* series, the exercises in the **Ready to Read** series involve the students actively. Proficient reading, like writing, requires a network of complex skills that can be taught, practiced, and improved. This series teaches competency in these skills by taking students on a step-by-step progression through the reading skills and word-attack strategies that promote efficient and effective reading. Those skills and strategies are then continuously recycled throughout the texts. Students read with a purpose, be it to increase reading efficiency, summarize an article, apply the skill presented in the chapter at hand, or review those skills presented in previous chapters.

We hope you find the exercises in this book useful for you and your students when they are **Ready to Read More**.

Acknowledgments

For their help in envisioning, supporting, and creating this series, we thank Laura Le Dréan, Lucille M. Kennedy, Dana Klinek, Diana George, and Shana McGuire at Longman as well as our friends, family, and colleagues: Tucker Aufranc; Daniel Blanchard; Diane Englund; Candace Kerner; Sharon McKay; Lynn Meng; Andrew Mountcastle; David, Matt, and Ian Root; and Bill Sherden.

Thanks also to the reviewers whose comments on early drafts of this book were very helpful: Marsha Abramovich, Tidewater Community College, Virginia Beach, VA; Martha Hall, The New England School of English, Cambridge, MA; Mary Jane Onnen, Glendale Community College, Glendale, AZ; and Cynthia Wiseman, CUNY–Borough of Manhattan Community College, New York, NY.

READY TO READ MORE

CHAPTER 1

Think Before You Read

I and The Village by Marc Chagall

About the Artist

The famous painter Marc Chagall (1887–1985) grew up in the small Russian village of Vitebsk. When he was a young man, Chagall moved to Paris, where he painted many of his best-known paintings, including *I and The Village*. Although he spent most of his life in France, he kept returning to Vitebsk in his mind and in his art. Chagall loved his native village and in this painting he looks back fondly at it. Although he is considered a modern artist, Chagall was inspired by the art of storytelling. In a way, this painting tells the story of life in a small village.

Look at the picture on page 2. Work with a partner and discuss the following questions.

1. Before you discuss Chagall's painting with your partner, talk about your hometown. What do you remember about it? Do you have pleasant memories? Why or why not? Make a list of words you would use to describe your hometown. Compare lists with a partner.

   _____   _____

   _____   _____

   _____   _____

2. Discuss what you know about life in small country villages. What kinds of things would you expect to see in a small country village?

   _____

   _____

   _____

3. Use the information about Marc Chagall and your own knowledge of hometowns and small villages to discuss the painting. What do you see? How does the painting make you feel?

   _____

   _____

   _____

> *When you thought about your own hometown and then discussed I and The Village, you used your background knowledge to help you understand the painting. Using your background knowledge is one of several strategies you can use to more easily understand things you see, hear, and read.*

Sharpen Your Reading Skills

Efficient readers use various strategies before, as, and after they read to help themselves understand and remember information. In this chapter, you will focus on strategies to use before you read. Following are several common prereading strategies that good readers use to prepare to read a text.

Before you begin to read, you should quickly perform several interrelated tasks:

1. Look over the text.

2. Think about what you already know about the topic.

3. Make predictions about the content.

4. Determine a purpose for reading.

The order in which you do the prereading tasks is not important. In fact some of these tasks may be done together, and some tasks may help prepare you to do an additional task. The important thing to remember is that if you take a few minutes to do these tasks, you will be in a better position to understand what you are going to read.

PREVIEW

Before you read, you should quickly look over, or **preview**, the material. If you are going to read an article or a textbook chapter, you should read the title and subtitle, section headings, words in bold print or italics, and introductions. You should also look at the pictures and graphics. Previewing is useful because it gives you an idea about the topic of the text and how it is organized.

ACTIVATE YOUR BACKGROUND KNOWLEDGE

You will understand what you read better if you connect the information with what you already know. The information you already know about a topic is called your **background knowledge**. Using your background knowledge will help you make connections while you read.

PREDICT

After you have previewed an article and thought about what you already know about the topic, you will be able to **make predictions**, or guesses, about what you are going to read. As you read, you can continue to make predictions about what will come next. Predicting before and while you read is important because it keeps you actively involved in reading and makes it easier for you to understand and remember what you read.

SET A PURPOSE

Before you read, it is helpful to **set a purpose** for reading. Having a purpose gives you a reason to read. It helps you read the text with a specific goal in mind. To set a purpose, you can ask yourself questions that you would like to have answered in the text. Then as you read the text, look for answers to the questions. Setting a purpose will help keep you actively involved in the reading process.

You probably already use these four skills in your everyday life. For example, imagine that you are visiting an amusement park such as Disney World for the first time. Before you start your day, you might take a look at a map of the park to get an idea of where the main attractions, restaurants, restrooms, and so on are located. Or you might take a quick walk around the park to get an idea of the layout (**Preview**). You might also think about other amusement parks you've been to and remember which things you had the most fun doing (**Activate Your Background Knowledge**). Then you will be in a position to guess (**Predict**) which attractions you would like to visit and make a plan for your day (**Set a Purpose**).

 Before you begin to read, take a few minutes to look over the text, think about what you already know about the topic, make predictions about the content, and determine a purpose for reading. This will help you understand what you read.

PRACTICE IN PREREADING

Use prereading strategies before you read the article on page 6.

1. Preview the article. Read the title and subtitle. Look at the picture and caption. Read the section headings.

2. Think about what you already know about the topic by discussing the following questions with a partner.
   a. Who is the oldest person you know?
   b. Why do you think some people live much longer than others?

3. Make predictions about the content of the article. Use the headings to predict which section in the article contains the following information. Write the correct heading from the article on the line.

Example

A Lifetime of Memories
_____

Some things Calment remembered from her long life

a. _____

Basic biographical information about the oldest person in history

b. _____

How Calment was able to live such a long life

c. _____

Achievements Calment made

d. _____

4. Determine your purpose for reading. Write two or three questions you would like the article to answer.

Example

What kind of exercise did she do?
_____

1. _____

2. _____

Now read the article on the next page to see if your predictions were accurate and if your questions were answered.

Meet the Oldest Person in History

A French Woman Sets a Record

Jeanne Louise Calment celebrated her 120th birthday in 1995.

Who Was the Oldest Person in the World?

1   Jeanne Louise Calment was born in Arles, France, on February 21, 1875, and lived there until her death on August 4, 1997. Her lifespan of 122 years 164 days is the longest reported for any person in history. She married her second cousin Fernand Calment in 1896 and survived both her only child and her only grandchild.

A Lifetime of Memories

2   No one had more memories than Jeanne Calment. She remembered when telephones were brand new: they were invented by Alexander Graham Bell in 1876, when Calment was a year old. She recalled visiting Paris as a child in the late 1880s and seeing the Eiffel Tower being built. As a young girl, she knew Vincent Van Gogh personally. She remembered the first rumblings of World War I in 1914. And she was already an old woman of 70 when World War II ended in 1945.

Making Records

3   When she was 120 years 238 days, Calment made it into the *Guinness Book of World Records* as the oldest person in recorded history. She beat the record of Shigechiyo Izumi of Japan, who died in 1986 at age 120 years 237 days. Calment said her achievement is no big deal. "It's not impressive at all," she said on her 120th birthday. "It's natural to grow old." That's true, but consider this: the average American woman lives to be 79. Living 41 years beyond that makes Calment "the Michael Jordan of aging," says Dr. Thomas Perls, an expert on old age at Harvard University. "The chances of you or me getting to be her age are similar to our chances of playing basketball like Jordan," says Perls. Calment made another record around the time of her 120th birthday. This one was a "rap" record called "Time's Mistress."

What Was Her Secret to Longevity?

4   What was Calment's secret? It helped that both her parents lived long lives (her mother died at 86, her father at 93). Doctors believe living long may run in families. Exercise and healthy habits also help. Calment was still riding her bicycle at 100! Sadly, a broken hip at 115 and loss of her eyesight made it hard for her to get around in her later years. Another key to long life is an upbeat spirit. Calment kept her sense of humor throughout her long life.

Be an Active Reader

READING 1: Reaching High and Living Long

BEFORE YOU READ

Activate Your Background Knowledge

A. What do you think are the five most important ways to help you live a long and healthy life? Write your ideas in the box, and then share your list with a partner. Write your partner's list in the box, and compare the two lists. Did you and your partner include any of the same ways? Did you include any way that your partner did not include?

Your List	Your Partner's List
1.	1.
2.	2.
3.	3.
4.	4.
5.	5.

B. Discuss the following questions with a partner.

1. Do you know anyone who has lived over a hundred years? Have you ever discussed the secret to his or her long life?

2. Have you ever had to overcome an obstacle to achieve a goal? What was your goal? What obstacle did you have to overcome?

Preview and Predict

C. Read the title and subtitle of the article on pages 9–10. Look at the picture and read the caption. Look at the headings. Can you predict what the article will be about? Think of three topics that might be discussed in the article. List the topics in the first three boxes in the left column of the Predict and Verify Chart.

Predict and Verify Chart	
Predict: Topics That Might be Discussed	Verify: Topics That Were Discussed

Preview the Vocabulary

D. The words in the box are boldfaced in the article. Complete the Vocabulary Chart with words from the box. If necessary, use your dictionary.

Words to Watch

diplomatic	centenarian	temper	segregation
outspoken	values	racism	
mix-up	struggle		

Vocabulary Chart	
Word	**Definition**
racism	unfair treatment of people, or violence against them, because they belong to a different race from yours
	good at dealing with people in a way that causes no bad feelings
	expressing your opinions honestly even if they shock or offend other people
	your ideas about what is right and wrong, or about what is important
	a mistake that causes confusion about details or arrangements
	to try very hard to achieve something, even though it is difficult
	the separation of one group of people from others because of race, sex, or religion
	a person who is at least 100 years old
	a tendency to become angry suddenly

You are going to read an article about two sisters who lived to be more than 100 years old. What do you want to find out about these women? Write two questions you would like the article to answer.

Example

How did the sisters live to be so old?

1. _____

2. _____

AS YOU READ

As you read, check to see if your predictions were accurate. Use the Verify column in the Predict and Verify Chart on page 8 to identify which of your predictions were confirmed in the article.

Reaching High and Living Long
Sisters Talk about Their Long and Productive Lives

1 Sarah Louise Delany and Anne Elizabeth Delany were two well-known sisters who both lived to be more than one hundred years old. Sarah Louise was better known as "Sadie," and Anne Elizabeth's nickname was "Bessie." When Bessie was 101 and Sadie was 103, they wrote a book about their lives called *Having Our Say: The Delany Sisters' First 100 Years.* Among other things, the sisters talked about their family life, personalities, and their careers as pioneering African American professionals.

The Delany sisters' book was a *New York Times* bestseller.

Different Personalities

2 Although they lived together for more than one hundred years, the two sisters had very different personalities. In *Having Our Say,* Sadie is described as sugar and Bessie as spice. Bessie openly wrote about her quick **temper** and strong opinions. Sadie, on the other hand, was calm, polite, and **diplomatic**. Sadie took to heart the old saying "You can catch more flies with honey than vinegar." Bessie admits that she was more like vinegar. The personality difference of the Delany sisters was evident in the way each one dealt with **racism**. During

(continued)

the postwar years, the sisters faced **segregation** laws in the South and unfair treatment in the North. Bessie was filled with anger at the unfair treatment of black Americans. She hated the Southern laws that made it illegal for black people to use the same drinking fountains, waiting rooms, and public bathrooms as whites. At times she was **outspoken** about injustice, even putting her life at risk. Sadie was much calmer about the effects of racism, yet she was often able to get what she wanted by acting sweet and innocent. She even figured out a way to get a teaching job at a white school by just showing up the first day and pretending that there had been a **mix-up** with the interview. Unlike Bessie, who often felt bitter about racism, Sadie was able to deal with problems in a more diplomatic way and appeared to suffer less. She wrote, "I never let prejudice stop me from what I wanted to do in this life."

Learning Values at Home

3   Sadie and Bessie were born in Raleigh, North Carolina, in 1889 and 1891 respectively. They grew up in a large and loving family on the campus of Saint Augustine's College in Raleigh. Their father, Henry Delany, was born a slave, but after years of hard work, he became the nation's first black Episcopal bishop and vice-principal of St. Augustine's College. Their mother, Nanny Delany, was a home economics* teacher at the college. Sadie and Bessie learned many **values** from their parents, including the importance of education. The Delanys brought up their children to "reach high" and to work hard to achieve their goals. All ten of their children went to college and became professionals. The Delanys also educated their children about the importance of helping others in the community. The children were taught, "Your job is to help somebody." All ten of the Delany children worked in service professions, helping people in need.

Reaching High as Professional Women

4   The Delany sisters' lives were full of hard-earned achievements. They **struggled** to achieve their goals during a time when most African Americans did not have educational or professional opportunities. After high school, they relocated to New York to attend Columbia University. Sadie earned bachelor's and master's degrees from Columbia Teachers College and became the city's first black home economics teacher. One of the first to integrate the New York school system, Sadie taught in the New York City public schools from 1920 to 1960. Bessie overcame obstacles caused by racism to become a dentist. She was admitted to dental school and became the second black woman to practice dentistry in New York. In all her years working as a dentist, Bessie never increased her rates, and she often treated her poorer patients for nothing.

Living a Long Life

5   Many people asked Sadie and Bessie about their secret to living so long. The two **centenarians** said that although there is no magic secret for living a long life, they followed several steps for having a healthy life. They ate seven vegetables and fruits every day, disapproved of tobacco, and never drank alcohol. They also stayed active by practicing yoga exercises and doing all their own housework. Neither sister married, joking that they never had husbands to "worry them to death." Another possible reason for their good health is that the sisters had a very close relationship and supported each other throughout their lives. They both loved reading, learning, and spending time with friends. Sadie's advice was "Life is short, and it's up to you to make it sweet." The extraordinary lives of Sadie and Bessie Delany continue to be an inspiration to people around the world.

---

*Home economics: the study of cooking, sewing, and other activities relating to the management of a home

AFTER YOU READ

Check Your Comprehension

A. True or false? Write T (True) or F (False) next to each of the following statements. If a statement is false, rewrite it to make it true.

> **Example**
>
> __F__ The two sisters had similar personalities. *The two sisters had very different personalities*

_____ 1. Sadie and Bessie learned many values from their parents such as the importance of education.

_____ 2. The sisters easily achieved their goals.

_____ 3. Bessie and Sadie both received college degrees and became professionals.

_____ 4. Bessie and Sadie grew up in a time when African Americans did not have many educational or professional opportunities.

_____ 5. The sisters had a magic secret for living a long life.

_____ 6. Both sisters dealt with prejudice and racism in the same way.

B. Compare answers to Exercise A with a partner. If you disagree on an answer, explain your reasons to your partner. Show your partner the sentence or sentences in the article that you used to decide if the statement was true or false.

Test Your Vocabulary

C. Complete each of the sentences that follow with the best word from the box. Be sure to use the correct form of the word.

> diplomatic   centenarian   temper   segregation
> outspoken   values   racism
> mix-up   struggle

1. Betsy doesn't like the mayor, and she is an _____ critic of his policies.

2. There was a _____ at the station and Eddie got on the wrong bus.

3. After Ronnie lost his job we had to _____ to pay our bills.

(continued)

4. My mother tries not to hurt anyone's feelings. She is a _____ person.

5. Both my grandmothers have lived to be over a hundred. They are _____.

6. Lilly's bad _____ often gets her into trouble. She needs to learn how to control it.

7. Most cities have laws prohibiting _____ in housing and education.

8. Our parents taught us the importance of family _____.

9. The police are sometimes accused of brutality and _____ toward black people.

Sum It Up

A summary is a short statement that gives the important ideas of a reading in your own words. Preparing a summary will help you remember the important information in the article.

Imagine that your friend has asked you to explain the article you just read, "Reaching High and Living Long." Make a list of the important ideas in the article. Then work in small groups and use the list to summarize the article for your group. Take turns summarizing the article for the other members of your group.

Important Ideas

_____

_____

_____

_____

Share Your Thoughts

A. Work in small groups to discuss these questions.

1. The sisters described Sadie as sugar and Bessie as spice. What do you think this means? Would you describe yourself as sugar or as spice? Why?

2. Sadie and Bessie ate lots of fruits and vegetables. What do you consider a healthy diet?

3. Sadie said, "Life is short, and it's up to you to make it sweet." What do you think she meant by this? Do you agree with her? Why or why not?

4. Sadie and Bessie practiced yoga. Have you ever done yoga? What kinds of exercise do you do? What are the benefits of regular exercise?

5. Sadie agreed with the old saying "You can catch more flies with honey than vinegar." What do you think this saying means? Do you have a similar one in your culture? Do you agree or disagree with the saying? Why?

6. The Delanys taught their children the importance of helping others in the community. Have you ever done any kind of community service? If so, what kind of service did you do?

B. Choose one of the questions in Exercise A and write a paragraph about it.

_____

_____

_____

_____

_____

READING 2: Living Past 100

BEFORE YOU READ

You have just read an article about two sisters who lived to be over 100 years old. Think about the fact that the Delany sisters lived very long lives. Now you are going to read an article about people in Okinawa, Japan, who also live very long lives.

Activate Your Background Knowledge

A. Work with a partner. Look at the map of Japan. Locate Okinawa on the map. Discuss these questions with your partner.

1. Have you ever been to Japan? What are your impressions of Japan?

2. Have you ever eaten at a Japanese restaurant? Did you enjoy the food? How is it similar to or different from the food in your native country? Do you think Japanese food is healthy? Why or why not?

Okinawa is a group of islands of Japan located in the East China Sea.

Preview and Predict

B. Preview the article on pages 16–18. Remember to look at the title, subtitle, headings, pictures, and the graph. Then make some predictions about the article. Write your predictions on the lines.

> **Example**
>
> the kinds of food Okinawans eat
> _____
>
> _____
>
> _____

Preview the Vocabulary

C. The words and phrases in the box are boldfaced in the article. Complete the Vocabulary Chart with words from the box. If necessary, use your dictionary.

> **Words to Watch**
>
> | | | | |
> |---|---|---|---|
> | nutrients | life expectancy | longevity | retirement |
> | martial arts | gene | connections | obesity |
> | ratio | positive attitude | | |

Vocabulary Chart	
Word	**Definition**
life expectancy	the length of time a person is expected to live
	being extremely fat in a way that is dangerous to one's health
	considering the good qualities of a situation or person and expecting success
	people you know who can help you
	a part of a cell that controls the development of a quality that is passed on to a living thing from its parents

Vocabulary Chart	
Word	**Definition**
	the time when you stop working
	sports such as karate in which you fight using your hands and feet
	chemicals or foods that help plants, animals, or people to live and grow
	long life
	a relationship between two amounts represented by numbers that show how much bigger one amount is than the other

Set a Purpose

Below is a chart called the KWL Chart. The K is for what you already KNOW about the topic, the W is for what you WANT to know, and the L is for what you LEARNED from the article after reading it.

D. Complete the first two columns of the KWL Chart before you read the article. Write what you know about the topic of Japanese living long lives in the first column. Write questions you would like to have answered in the second column. You will fill in the third column after you read the article.

KWL Chart		
What I Know (K)	**What I Want to Know (W)**	**What I Learned (L)**

AS YOU READ

As you read the article, verify the predictions you wrote in Exercise B.

Living Past 100
Okinawans Outlive Everyone Else

Impressive Facts

1   Are you one of the many people who want to know how you can live a longer and healthier life? If you are, you could learn some valuable lessons by studying the lifestyle of a group of Japanese people. Japanese people live longer than anyone else in the world. And the people who live on the Japanese islands of Okinawa live longer than anyone else in Japan. Here are the amazing facts. According to the Japanese government, 457 Okinawans are at least 100 years old. That means for every 100,000 people who live on the islands, there are 34.7 centenarians. That's the highest **ratio** in the world. Compared to the United States, where there are only 10 centenarians for every 100,000 people, it's a big difference. Okinawans have a saying: "At 70 you are still a child, at 80 a young man or woman. And if at 90 someone from Heaven invites you over, tell him: 'Just go away, and come back when I am 100.'" In fact, the average **life expectancy** is 81.2 years on Okinawa. For an Okinawan woman the average is 86, and the average man lives to 78.

Studying the Secret of a Long Life

2   Okinawans are considered to be the healthiest people on the planet. They often live healthy, active, independent lives well into their nineties and hundreds. They generally have fewer health problems as they age. For example, their rates of **obesity**, heart disease, memory loss, and several kinds of cancer are far below those in the United States and other industrialized countries. What is their secret to **longevity**? Three doctors have been trying to answer the question. A Japanese doctor, Dr. Makoto Suzuki, has been studying the Okinawans for over 25 years. He has researched the health and life-style of 676 subjects. Canadian Dr. Bradley J. Willcox and his twin brother, Dr. Craig Willcox, have also been involved in the research. Together they have written two books about their research: *The Okinawa Program* and *The Okinawa Diet Plan*. According to these doctors, several factors, including good **genes**, help Okinawans to live such long and healthy lives. Three of the most important factors are diet, exercise, and life-style.

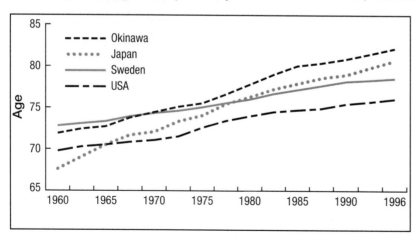

Life Expectancy in Long-Lived Populations and the United States

Eating a Healthy Diet

3   The Okinawans eat a diet that is rich in fruits, vegetables, soy, grains, and fish. In fact, about 90% of the traditional Okinawan diet consists of sweet potatoes, soy-based foods, whole grains, fruits, and vegetables. Most Okinawans eat lots of tofu, a soft white food that is made from soybeans. Tofu and other soy products contain **nutrients** believed to fight cancer and heart disease. Okinawans also drink six glasses of water and lots of green tea every day. Drinking green tea has many health benefits. Finally, Okinawans don't overeat. They stop eating before they are full. They call this *hara hachi bu*, which means you stop eating when you feel 80 percent full.

Getting Lots of Exercise

4   On Okinawa, elderly people lead active lives. They act and look younger than their years. For exercise, Okinawans work in their gardens, ride bicycles, and take long walks. Many older Okinawans still practice **martial arts** like tai chi and karate. Dancing is a favorite form of activity among Okinawans, too. Traditional Okinawan dances are still very popular.

Having a Positive Attitude

5   Okinawans believe that a **positive attitude** about life can help you look younger, feel better, and live longer. It can also help reduce stress. Since stress can cause sickness and make people age more quickly, Okinawans have learned to be experts at reducing stress in their lives. One of the most important things they do to reduce stress is live life at a slower pace. They also have lots of friends and social **connections**. An Okinawan proverb says, "One cannot live in

Many Okinawans are healthy and active in their 90s.

this world without the support of others." Okinawans stay connected with each other throughout their lives. Research shows that people with lots of social connections usually live longer than people without strong connections to family or friends. The social connections form a network of

Many older Okinawans practice martial arts.

support. Okinawans help each other. Another proverb says, "If one earnestly makes efforts for the sake of another, soon these efforts will

(continued)

be for the sake of yourself." Although many older Okinawans live alone, they rely on support from people in their communities. This support enables them to live independently in their own homes. Having a purpose in life is also important. In fact, there is no word for **retirement** in the Okinawan language. People work as long as they are able and have a sense of contributing to the community.

AFTER YOU READ

Complete the KWL chart

A. Fill in the third column in the KWL Chart on page 15. Write down information you learned from reading the article. Did the article answer any of your questions from the second column? Which ones? Look at the things you wrote in the first column. Were any of your ideas confirmed or rejected in the article? Which ones?

B. Work in small groups. Use your KWL Charts to discuss what you learned from the article with your classmates.

Check Your Comprehension

C. Work with a partner and follow the steps.

1. On a separate piece of paper, write two questions for each paragraph in the article. Use questions words such as *who, what, when, where, why, how many,* and so on. On the back of the paper, write the answers to your questions.

> **Example**
>
> What is the average life expectancy for women on Okinawa?

2. Now exchange your questions with your partner and answer the questions your partner wrote.

3. Check the answers your partner wrote for your questions. Are your partner's answers the same as the ones you wrote on the back of your paper?

Sharpen Your Vocabulary Skills

WORD PARTS

You can improve your vocabulary skills by learning about the structure of words and how they are formed in English. Many English words are made up of several parts called *prefixes*, *roots*, and *suffixes*. For example, the word *unfriendly* has three parts. The main part of the word, *friend*, is called the root. The prefix *un-* and the suffix *-ly* make *friend* into the word *unfriendly*.

Prefixes

One strategy you can use to figure out the meaning of an unfamiliar word is to look at its prefix.

> A **prefix** is a group of letters that is added to the beginning of a word to make another word. The prefix changes the meaning of the word. For example, adding the prefix **dis-** to the verb **approve** makes the verb **disapprove**, which means "not to approve."
> I disapprove of drinking and driving.

Negative Prefixes

English has several prefixes that change a word to its opposite or mean *no* or *not*.

Negative Prefixes		
Prefix	Meaning	Example
dis-	*not*	disobey
il-, im-, in-, ir-	*not*	illegal, impractical, inappropriate, irrational
mis-	*badly, wrongly*	misuse
non-	*not*	nonsense
un-	*not*	unable

Not all prefixes change a word to its opposite, but all prefixes change the word in some way. Study the following chart to learn some more common prefixes. Learning these prefixes will help you expand your vocabulary.

Common Prefixes

Prefix	Meaning	Example
anti-	*opposed to, against*	antifreeze
bi-	*two, twice*	bilingual, biannual
extra-	*outside, beyond*	extraterrestrial, extraordinary
over-	*too much, additional*	overcharge, overtime
post-	*after*	postgraduate, postpone
pre-	*before*	prewar, preview
re-	*again, back*	rewrite, redo, rewind
semi-	*half, partly*	semicircle, semiprecious
sub-	*under, below, less important*	substandard, subway, subcommittee
super-	*larger, greater, more powerful*	superhuman, supermarket
trans-	*between two things, across*	transatlantic, transportation
en-, em-	*to make something have a quality*	enlarge, empower

A. Add the correct prefix to the root word in each of the following sentences.

dis- bi- over-

1. The magazine comes out every two weeks. It's a _____**biweekly**_____ (weekly) publication.

2. The cake tastes dry. I must have _____ (cooked) it.

3. My son won't eat spinach, carrots, or peas. In fact, he _____ (likes) most vegetables.

anti- semi- post-

4. She's not really _____ (social). She's just very shy.

5. Our team is playing in the _____ (finals).

6. She wants to do _____ (graduate) work at McGill University.

non- trans- pre-

7. This is a _____ (smoking) area.

8. The first _____ (continental) railroad in the United States was completed in 1869.

9. Before you write an essay, it's helpful to do some _____ (writing) activities such as brainstorming.

un- extra- re-

10. Before I take the test, I'm going to _____ (view) my notes.

11. Use your key to _____ (lock) the lock.

12. I like to take part in _____ (curricular) activities after school.

mis- sub- super-

13. Many cartoon characters have _____ (human) powers.

14. We usually take the _____ (way) to work.

15. The child got into trouble for _____ (behaving) in class.

B. Work with a partner. Look at the following list of words from the articles "Reaching High and Living Long" and "Living Past 100." Identify the prefix in each word and discuss how it changes the meaning of the word. Then think of other words with the same prefix. Complete the chart below. Finally, join another group and compare your lists.

Word	Prefix	Meaning	Other words
unable	un-	not	untrue, unreliable, unlock
injustice			
prejudice			
relocate			
postwar			
unfair			
illegal			
extraordinary			
disapprove			
enable			
overeat			

Share Your Thoughts

Okinawans have many sayings, proverbs, and customs. Work in small groups to discuss the proverbs and customs mentioned in the article.

1. "At 70 you are still a child, at 80 a young man or woman. And if at 90 someone from Heaven invites you over, tell him: 'Just go away, and come back when I am 100.'"

2. "If one earnestly makes efforts for the sake of another, soon these efforts will be for the sake of yourself."

3. Okinawans practice *hara hachi bu*, which means you stop eating when you feel 80 percent full.

Explore the Web

Work with a partner. Use the Internet to do some research about healthy diets. Use a search engine such as Google. Type in a few key words such as "healthy + diets." Use the information to plan three healthy meals. Join another pair of students and compare your meals.

Breakfast	Lunch	Dinner

Go Beyond the Text

1. Look back at the list you made on page 7 of the five most important ways to help you live a long and healthy life. Do you still agree with those ideas? What other ideas would you add?

2. Work with a group of three or four students. Discuss your ideas and work together to make a new list of five important ways to help you live a long and healthy life.

3. Use the list to make and illustrate a poster like the example below. Think of a title for your poster and write it on the top. Share your poster with the whole class.

How to Live a Long and Healthy Life

1. Get lots of exercise.

CHAPTER 2

Identify Main Ideas

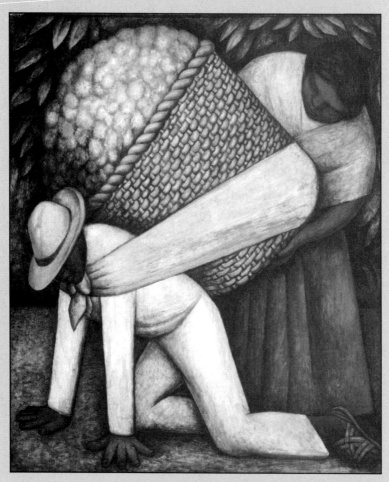

The Flower Carrier by Diego Rivera

About the Artist

Diego Rivera was born in Guanajuato, Mexico in 1886 and is considered one of Mexico's greatest and most influential artists. As a young man, he traveled to Paris, France, to study and work with a group of young artists. When he returned to Mexico in 1921, he painted large murals with themes that dealt with the life, history, and social problems of Mexico. Rivera's goal was to create paintings that would speak directly to the common people. *The Flower Carrier* is one of Rivera's most famous paintings.

Look at the painting by Diego Rivera on page 24. Discuss it with a partner and then answer the questions.

1. What is the painting about? What are the people doing? What are they wearing? How do you think they feel?

   _____

   _____

2. What do you think Diego Rivera wants you to know about the people in the painting?

   _____

   _____

When you decided what Rivera wanted you to know about the flower carrier, you identified the main idea. The strategy of identifying the main idea is also important in reading.

Sharpen Your Reading Skills

IDENTIFYING THE MAIN IDEA

Identifying the main idea of a text is one of the most important reading strategies used by good readers. Identifying the main idea will help you understand and remember what you read. Ask yourself these two questions to find the main idea.

1. **"Who or what is the reading about?"** The answer will be the **topic.** The topic is the word or phrase that tells what the reading is about. The topic of Diego Rivera's painting is *flower carriers.* To help identify the topic, look for a word or phrase that is repeated. Or pretend that you have to use one word or a short phrase to tell someone what a reading is about.

2. **"What does the author want me to know about the topic?"** The answer to this question is the main idea. In the painting, the main idea is *The flower carriers are working hard.*

FINDING THE TOPIC AND MAIN IDEA OF A PARAGRAPH

Most English writing is organized into paragraphs. A paragraph is a group of sentences that are related to each other because they are all about the same general topic. The main idea of the paragraph is the author's most important point about the topic. Sometimes the author states the main idea in one sentence called the **topic sentence.**

 The topic sentence is often the first sentence of a paragraph, but it can also be the last sentence or a sentence in the middle of the paragraph.

Dictionaries are full of information about words. There are thousands of words listed in a dictionary. The dictionary tells you how to spell and pronounce each word correctly and also tells you the meaning of each word. Many words in English have more than one meaning, and the dictionary gives you all the meanings. The dictionary also gives you the part of speech (noun, verb, adjective, and so on) of each word.

Ask: "Who or what is the paragraph about?" Answer: Dictionaries

Ask: "What does the author want me to know about the topic?" Underline: Dictionaries are full of information about words.

Now work with a partner to find the topic and main idea of each the following paragraphs. Ask yourselves, "Who or what is the paragraph about?" (This is the topic.) Then ask yourselves, "What does the author want me to know about the topic?" Work together to find the sentence that states the main idea. Underline it.

1. The twentieth century Mexican artist Frida Kahlo was born on July 6, 1907. She was very rebellious as a child and often got into trouble at school. While still a student, Frida suffered serious injuries and many broken bones in a bus accident and almost died. This experience inspired Frida to begin painting. She expressed her pain and suffering in her artwork. A few years after the accident, Kahlo married Diego Rivera, another famous Mexican artist. It was a marriage with many problems that eventually led to a divorce, but the couple later remarried. Frida Kahlo experienced much pain in her life, but her art continues to inspire people all over the world.

Topic: _____

2. One of the most famous symbols of American independence is the Liberty Bell. During the colonial period, the bell was hung in Philadelphia in 1753. It was made in England, and the words "Proclaim liberty throughout all the land" were written on it. On July 4, 1776, when the colonial leaders issued the Declaration of Independence, they rang the Liberty Bell. Every year afterwards, the Liberty Bell was rung on the Fourth of July to celebrate American Independence. In 1846, a crack developed on the side of the bell, so it could no longer ring. The Liberty Bell is still in Philadelphia, and thousands of visitors still visit it when touring the historical city.

Topic: _____

3.   Many cities all over the world have parks where people can go to relax. The first urban park in the United States was New York City's Central Park. Covering 843 acres, it is the largest park in New York City. The city bought the land for Central Park in 1856. The men who designed the park, Frederick Law Olmsted and Calvert Vaux, wanted to create a public park where people could enjoy nature in one of the busiest and biggest cities in the world. As a result of their planning, Central Park includes many ponds, gardens, and walking paths. It also includes a zoo, playgrounds, and even a skating rink. Although Central Park is an important tourist attraction, it is first a place where New Yorkers go to run, bicycle, visit with friends, bird watch, or sit quietly and read. Just as Olmsted and Vaux hoped, Central Park is a place where people go to escape the busy and crowded atmosphere of the city and enjoy the beauty of nature.

Topic: _____

4.   Most people need eight hours of sleep in order to learn, remember, and problem-solve effectively. Yet many people do not get enough sleep. If you are among the millions of people who have trouble sleeping, there are several things you can do to help your body get the kind of rest it requires. First of all, eat nutritious foods and get lots of exercise during the day. Second, avoid stimulants like coffee, cola drinks, tea, and chocolate, especially in the evening. Try to go to sleep at the same time every night. Drink a glass of warm milk at bedtime, or take a warm bath to help you relax. Last but not least, sleep might come more easily if your mattress and pillow are comfortable, your room is quiet, and the temperature is satisfactory.

Topic: _____

5.   Mother Teresa was born on August 27, 1910. Originally named Agnes, she was born into an Albanian family but spent most of her life in India. As a young girl she decided to become a missionary, and at age 18 she left home to join a convent in Calcutta, India. At first she worked as a teacher in a religious school, but then she decided to go out into the streets to help the poor and those with serious illnesses such as leprosy and AIDS. Mother Teresa established a hospice where people who were dying could come to spend their last days in peace. In addition, she founded an orphanage for children. Mother Teresa received the Nobel Peace Prize in 1979 for her compassionate service and dedication to humanity. Mother Teresa will always be remembered as a woman who spent her life helping the poor and sick.

Topic: _____

FINDING UNSTATED MAIN IDEAS

It is not always easy to identify the main idea. Sometimes, the author does not state the main idea directly in a topic sentence. In that case, you must use all the information in the paragraph to figure out the main idea yourself.

Use the information in each of the following paragraphs to figure out the main idea. Circle the letter of the statement that best expresses the main idea. Then compare choices with a partner.

Example

As many of us have learned the hard way, it is not fun to be stung by a bee. Luckily, you don't have to stay indoors all the time to avoid getting stung. One way to avoid bee stings is to wear light-colored clothing because bees like dark colors. Don't forget to wear shoes to protect the bottoms of your feet—bees don't discriminate as to where they sting you. Also do not wear perfume or any other sweet-smelling body or hair scents or you'll find yourself a magnet for bees. If you are eating, keep your food covered. If you are drinking fruit juice, soda, or any other sweet drink, be very careful and check the inside of the can or bottle before you take a drink. You do not want to get stung on the inside of your mouth. If bees start coming around, do not jump up and start dancing around. You will be safer from a sting if you don't move. If you are picking flowers to take inside, make sure you aren't taking any bees inside with you.

a. There are several ways to protect yourself from getting stung by a bee.
b. Since bees like dark colors, you can avoid getting stung if you wear light-colored clothing.
c. Although it's not fun to be stung by a bee, bees provide a valuable service to nature.

Explanation

- Choice *a.* is correct because it best expresses the main idea of the whole paragraph.
- Choice *b.* cannot be the main idea because it expresses only one point in the paragraph, not its most important idea.
- Choice *c.* is incorrect because the paragraph never states that bees provide a valuable service to nature.

1. Each year stores around the world lose billions of dollars to shoplifting, or the stealing of merchandise by shoppers. To reduce this problem, store managers hire plainclothes security guards who pretend to be ordinary shoppers but actually watch other shoppers to check for stealing. Hidden cameras are also used in many stores for security purposes. Some stores follow the policy that anyone who is caught shoplifting must pay a fine of five times the cost of the shoplifted items. In many cases, the store management calls the police and the shoplifter is arrested. Because of the billions of dollars lost to shoplifting and the high cost of security, shoplifting is a costly problem for stores. Therefore, stores must increase prices for everyone, including the honest customers.

a. Shoplifting is a serious problem for stores around the world.
b. Many stores use hidden cameras for security purposes.
c. Clothing stores lose the most money to shoplifting.

2. Everything seems to be getting more expensive these days. One exception, though, is the public library. Public libraries are free and open to the public. Not only do libraries have books, but they also have magazines, newspapers, videos, CDs, and DVDs. The librarians help people to do research and find information in many sources. Some libraries offer free literacy tutoring for helping adults to learn how to read. Most libraries have wonderful programs for children, including story hours and special children's performances. Libraries are important community centers. In addition, they may also have speakers, poetry readings, musical concerts, and other types of events. The entrances to most libraries have bulletin boards with notices from different groups in the area, such as announcements of local performances, clubs, and public services.

   a. Everything seems to be getting more expensive these days.
   b. In many ways, libraries are of great value to the community.
   c. The Free Library of Philadelphia is the oldest library in the United States.

3. One of the first civilizations in history arose in a place called Mesopotamia. This early civilization was called Sumer. From about 4000 B.C. to 2000 B.C., the Sumerians developed a rich and sophisticated society. They made the first wheels, sailboats, irrigation canals, and plows. The Sumerians were also skilled mathematicians and astronomers. They developed many ways of understanding time. They even had an accurate calendar. Perhaps the Sumerians are best known for devising the first form of writing, called cuneiform.

   a. Cuneiform was the first form of writing.
   b. The Sumerian civilization had many important achievements.
   c. The Sumerians were the most important ancient civilization.

4. Most people know that red roses mean love. But did you know that yellow roses mean friendship? Roses aren't the only kind of flower that has a special meaning. In fact, some people say that flowers have a language of their own. For example, orchids mean beauty and delicacy. Bells of Ireland symbolize good luck. Hope and inspiration can be expressed by sending someone irises. Lilies are for celebration and goldenrod for success.

   a. Red can mean love or friendship.
   b. Flowers are beautiful.
   c. Different kinds of flowers have different meanings.

5. Secondary sources are descriptions of past events written by people after the events happened. A history of the Russian Revolution of 1917 written in 2004 is a secondary source. Secondary sources include textbooks, biographies, and encyclopedias; magazine, newspaper, and journal articles; and websites on the Internet. Historians use secondary sources to answer some of their questions about the past, but they also look for primary sources. Primary sources are descriptions of past events created at the time of the event. A personal letter from a Russian

(continued)

person written in 1917 that describes the events going on at that time is an example of a primary source. Other examples of primary sources include government and church records, diaries and journals, maps, photographs and paintings, and artifacts such as coins and pieces of clothing. Historians can get valuable information about past events by studying primary sources.

a. Historians get their information from two different kinds of sources: primary and secondary.
b. Government records have more valuable information than personal letters or diaries.
c. Textbooks and encyclopedias are secondary source materials.

 Look for the author's main idea(s) when you read. The main idea is the author's most important point about the topic and answers the question, "What is the main point that the author is making about the topic?" To find the main idea, you need to identify the topic and then ask yourself, "What does the author want me to know about the topic?"

PRACTICE WITH MAIN IDEAS

Use prereading strategies before you read the article "Silk: The Queen of Textiles."

1. Preview the article. Read the title and subtitle. Look at the picture and caption. Read the section headings.

2. Think about what you already know about the topic.

3. Make predictions about the content of the article. Use the headings to predict which section contains the following information. Write the correct heading on the line.

a. _____

The process of silk making

b. _____

Current information about the silk industry

c. _____

A general description of silk

d. _____

Information about the history of silk

4. Set a purpose for reading by writing three questions you would like the article to answer.

a. _____

b. _____

c. _____

5. As you read the article, look for the main idea of each section. Write the main idea on the line.

6. After you read the article, compare main ideas with a partner.

Silk: The Queen of Textiles

Making silk [cloth] is a complicated process.

What Is Silk?

1   Silk is a natural fiber that is used to make a smooth and shiny cloth. Many people consider silk the most beautiful of all textile fibers, and it is often called the queen of textiles. Silk cloth is used to make clothing because it is soft, sheer, and lightweight but strong. It is also long-lasting and can be dyed beautiful colors. Silk is a comfortable fabric to wear and keeps you warm in cold weather and cool in the summer.

Main idea: _____

How Is Silk Made?

2   Silk is made from the cocoons of tiny insects called silkworms. Silkworm caterpillars are kept in special containers where they are fed a special diet of mulberry leaves. After four to six weeks, the silkworm caterpillars spin cocoons made of long threads and begin to turn into adult silkworm moths. At this point, the cocoons are steamed and dipped in boiling water to kill the moths. Finally, the threads of the cocoons are unraveled and are ready to be woven into cloth. Thousands of silkworms are needed to produce enough silk for just one dress or shirt. As you can see, the process of making silk is time-consuming and complicated.

Main idea: _____

A Long and Colorful History

3   Silk has a long and colorful history, beginning in China around 3000 B.C. According to an old legend, the Empress Xi Ling discovered silk by accident. One day as she was sitting under a mulberry tree drinking tea, a cocoon fell into her cup. When she removed the cocoon, she noticed that it had started to unwind. The Empress was impressed at the beauty of the threads. As the story goes, Xi Ling's accidental discovery led to the beginning of the silk industry in China. Whether the legend is true or not, the production of silk first took place in China. The beauty and value of silk were quickly appreciated, and it became one of the most prized products of the ancient world. But for thousands of years the Chinese kept the secret of how to make silk. Silk was sold to other countries, but the knowledge of how

(continued)

to make it was highly guarded. Since only the Chinese knew the secret of how to make the precious fabric, silk was very valuable for trade. Chinese merchants traveled thousands of miles to sell and trade silk. They traveled west through China to India, Persia, and cities in the Roman Empire on a route that came to be called the Silk Road. During the eleventh century European traders stole several silkworm eggs and seeds of a mulberry tree. With these, they began raising silkworms in Europe.

Main idea: _____

The Silk Industry Today

4 Although artificial fibers like nylon and polyester have replaced silk in much of the textile industry, silk is still a big industry. Over 60,000 tons of raw silk are produced annually to be made into shirts, dresses, bed sheets, curtains, and other products. Most silk today is produced in China and a few other countries including Japan, India, and Italy. In China 10 million farmers grow silkworms, and another half million make silk fabrics. The silk industry has a commercial value of $200–$500 million annually.

Main idea: _____

Be an Active Reader

READING 1: The Silk Road

BEFORE YOU READ

Preview the Article

A. Read the title and subtitle of the article on pages 34–35. Ask yourself, "How can trade connect people who live far away from each other?" Look at the map and the picture. Read the captions. Have you ever been to any of the places on the map? Do you know anything about any of the places? Have you ever seen or ridden a camel? How can camels help people who are traveling? Look at the five headings and remember that they give you clues about the content of each paragraph in the article.

Activate Your Background Knowledge and Make Predictions

B. You have already read an article about silk. You learned that silk was a precious fabric that was very valuable for trade. Discuss what you already know about the Silk Road. Use the information that you gained from previewing the article and your personal knowledge to make some predictions about the content.

_____

_____

_____

C. The words and phrases in the box are boldfaced in the article. Complete the Vocabulary Chart with words from the box. If necessary, use your dictionary.

Words to Watch

route	merchant	caravan	no longer
thieves	hazardous	goods	geography
destination	decline	link	

Vocabulary Chart

Word	Definition
	a group of people, with animals or vehicles, who travel together
	dangerous
	someone who buys and sells goods
	a gradual decrease in the quality, quantity, or importance of something
	products; things that are produced to be sold
	a connection between events, people, or ideas
	the place that someone or something is going to
	people who steal things
	the way from one place to another
	meaning that something happened in the past but does not happen now
	natural features of a place, such as mountains, rivers, deserts

Set a Purpose

You are going to read about the Silk Road. What do you want to find out about this ancient trade route? Write two questions you would like the article to answer.

1. _____

2. _____

As you read the article, complete the Main Idea Chart on page 36.

The Silk Road

Connecting the People of Asia and Europe through Trade

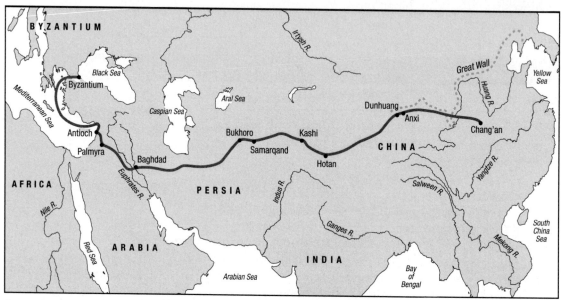

Connecting East and West, from China to Rome, the Silk Road linked distant cultures for almost 2,000 years.

An Important Ancient Trade Route

1   The Silk Road is the name given to an ancient trade **route** connecting Europe and Asia. One of the world's oldest and most historically important trade routes, the Silk Road began around 100 B.C. when Chinese **merchants** traveled across Asia to trade and sell silk and other products in the Roman Empire. The Silk Road provided a **link** between distant cultures for almost 2,000 years. As people traveled along the Silk Road, they traded **goods** and exchanged ideas. The Silk Road wasn't just a single road; it was a network of trade routes through cities in Asia. Merchants traveled along the Silk Road with their goods and camels in **caravans**, but they rarely traveled the whole distance of the Silk

Road. Instead, they moved along the Silk Road from one trading center to another. When the merchants arrived at a new town they did more than just trade goods. They ate, drank, and socialized. They learned about each other's similarities and differences. Some told stories about the places they had been to and gave each other information about travel conditions along the Silk Road.

Dangers along the Road

2   Travel along the Silk Road was not easy, and merchants faced many difficulties along the way. A combination of harsh climate, difficult **geography**, and the threat of attacks made

the road **hazardous** at all times of year. Caravans often had to cross the hot dry deserts of Central Asia with no water for miles. They also had to travel through some of the highest mountains in the world, which was challenging and dangerous. In addition to heavy snow and flooding of the mountain passes, traders also had to worry about **thieves** who were ready to attack them and steal their goods.

More Than Silk Was Traded

3   Although the Silk Road got its name from the valuable silk fabric that traders carried from China to Europe, many other products were traded as well. Furs, tea, spices, and jewels also moved from East to West, making traders wealthy. However, it wasn't a one-way road. Silver, gold, ivory, jade, carpets, cosmetics, and glass moved along the Silk Road in the opposite direction, from Europe, Asia, Arabia, and Africa.

Traders used camels to carry their goods along the Silk Road.

The Exchange of Ideas between Cultures

4   The story of the Silk Road involved more than just trade and silk. As people traveled along the Silk Road, they also carried ideas with them and made connections with other cultures. The earliest travelers brought their own languages and cultures. They learned about each other's customs, beliefs, religions, and philosophies. Many important scientific ideas and technical discoveries traveled along the Silk Road too. They included gunpowder, the magnetic compass, paper-making and glass-making, and the printing press. People on the Silk Road exchanged ideas in much the same way we do when we travel today. In a way, the Silk Road was the information superhighway of its time.

The Silk Road Today

5   The Silk Road lasted until the fifteenth century when a sea route from Europe to Asia was discovered. Since sea trade was safer, less expensive, and faster and ships could carry more goods than camels could, the Silk Road gradually fell into **decline**. Although the Silk Road **no longer** exists as a trade route, sites along its route have become popular tourist **destinations**. Travel companies offer all kinds of tours that you can take to explore the Silk Road. A good tour will help you discover the beauty of places on the Silk Road and learn about the history and achievements of civilizations along the way.

Main Idea Chart
Paragraph 1 Main idea: _____ _____
Paragraph 2 Main idea: _____ _____
Paragraph 3 Main idea: _____ _____
Paragraph 4 Main idea: _____ _____
Paragraph 5 Main idea: _____ _____

AFTER YOU READ

Compare Main Idea Charts

A. Compare Main Idea Charts with a partner. Did you identify the same main idea for each section? If not, reread the paragraph and ask yourselves, "What is the topic of the paragraph?" and "What does the author want me to know about the topic?"

Check Your Comprehension

B. True or false? Write T (True) or F (False) next to each of the following statements. If a statement is false, rewrite it to make it true.

_____ 1. The Silk Road was used only for selling and trading silk.

_____ 2. People usually traveled the whole distance of the Silk Road.

_____ 3. Several factors made travel along the Silk Road dangerous.

_____ 4. The Silk Road connected distant cultures for almost 2,000 years.

_____ 5. Today tourists can explore the sites along the ancient Silk Road.

_____ 6. The discovery of sea routes caused the decline of the Silk Road.

_____ 7. Merchants rarely socialized with each other along the Silk Road.

Test Your Vocabulary

c. Complete each of the sentences that follow with the best word from the box. Be sure to use the correct form of the word.

route	merchants	caravan	no longer
thieves	hazardous	goods	geography
destination	decline	link	

1. There were many reasons for the _____ and fall of the Roman Empire.

2. They produce leather _____ like wallets, handbags, and briefcases.

3. What is the shortest _____ from Charleston to Atlanta?

4. Today the Internet provides a _____ among people all over the world.

5. Mr. Allen _____ works for the company. Now he has his own business.

6. The _____ traveled safely through the mountain passes.

7. _____ traded products and ideas all along the Silk Road.

8. The _____ stole $15,000 and several valuable pieces of jewelry.

9. The Eiffel Tower is a popular tourist _____ in Paris.

10. Be careful! The ice and snow make this a _____ road in the winter.

11. We learned about the climate and _____ of Korea.

Sum It Up

Remember that a summary is a short statement that gives the important ideas of a reading in your own words. Use your Main Idea Chart on page 36 to help you write a one-paragraph summary of the article. Remember to include only main ideas from the article in your summary.

_____

_____

_____

_____

Share Your Thoughts

A. Work in small groups to discuss these questions.

1. Why was the Silk Road important to the ancient world? How did it act as a link between cultures?

2. Do you think the Silk Road was more important for the exchange of goods or for the exchange of ideas? Why?

3. Do you think the Silk Road was as important in the past as the Internet is today? Explain your answer.

B. Choose one of the questions in Exercise A and write a paragraph about it.

_____

_____

_____

_____

_____

READING 2: Yo-Yo Ma and the Silk Road Project

BEFORE YOU READ

You have just read an article about the ancient Silk Road. You learned that as people traveled along the Silk Road, they not only traded goods, but perhaps more important, they exchanged ideas. Now you are going to read an article about the world famous cello player, Yo-Yo Ma, and his new project that was inspired by the ancient Silk Road.

Activate Your Background Knowledge

A. Discuss these questions with a partner.

1. What kinds of music do you usually listen to? What kinds of music are most popular in your native country? Do you enjoy listening to the traditional music of your native culture?

2. Do you ever listen to music from other cultures? In what ways do you think music can be a link between cultures?

3. How often do you attend music concerts? Who performed at the last concert you attended?

4. Look at the picture on page 41 of Yo-Yo Ma playing a cello. Have you heard of him? Have you ever heard any of his music? Discuss what you already know about Yo-Yo Ma.

Preview and Predict

B. Preview the article on pages 41–42. Remember to look at the title, subtitle, headings, and pictures. Then make some predictions about the article. Write your predictions on the lines.

_____

_____

_____

Preview the Vocabulary

C. The words and phrases in the box are boldfaced in the article. Complete the Vocabulary Chart with words from the box. If necessary, use your dictionary.

> **Words to Watch**
>
> inspiration   liberal arts   diversity
> legend   showcase   contribution
> global   collaborate   cross-cultural

Vocabulary Chart	
Word	**Definition**
	subjects that increase someone's general knowledge rather than teach technical skills
	affecting the whole world, or relating to the whole world
	someone who is famous and admired for being extremely good at doing something
	to work together for a special purpose
	belonging to or involving two or more societies, countries, or cultures
	something that is given or done to help something else be a success
	a range of different people or things; variety
	to exhibit the good qualities of a person, organization
	something or someone that encourages you to do or produce something good

Set a Purpose

You are going to read an article about Yo-Yo Ma and his Silk Road Project. Write two questions you would like the article to answer.

1. _____

2. _____

Look for the main idea of each paragraph. Underline the sentence or sentences that describe the main idea of the paragraph.

Yo-Yo Ma and the Silk Road Project
A Musician's Contribution to World Harmony

Cultural Inspiration for Artists

1   Throughout history, artists have looked to foreign cultures for **inspiration**. Many of the world's greatest painters, musicians, and writers have been influenced by ancient cultures and foreign traditions. The world-famous cellist Yo-Yo Ma is one of those artists. His effort to explore artistic and cultural differences resulted in the Silk Road Project. This project involves a cultural exchange of music and other art forms among countries of the Silk Road, an ancient trade route linking Asia and Europe. Countries represented in the Silk Road Project include China, Japan, Korea, Mongolia, Uzbekistan, Tajikistan, Azerbaijan, Pakistan, India, Iran, Armenia, and Italy.

Origins of the Silk Road

2   The network of trade routes called the Silk Road existed for almost 2,000 years. Traders traveled along the Silk Road carrying goods to and from China, Central Asia, and the lands along the Mediterranean Sea. In their journeys, the traders brought not only products

Cellist Yo-Yo Ma dreamed of finding a way to celebrate cultural diversity through music.

but also new ideas and customs to the distant regions of the Silk Road. Religions, scientific inventions, and different forms of music and art spread across several continents.

A Musician's Dream

3   The idea of the Silk Road has fascinated people for centuries. Recently, it captured the imagination of a musician named Yo-Yo Ma. Cellist Yo-Yo Ma dreamed of an organization that would **showcase** the different cultures of the Silk Road region and remember its spirit of international cooperation. Ma was born in France in 1955 to Chinese parents. He immigrated to the United States as a child and soon became a musical **legend**. Ma was already a world-famous cellist by the time he was a teenager. He decided to attend Harvard University instead of a music school in order to obtain a broader **liberal arts** education. By 2004, he had won fifteen Grammy awards* for his recordings of the cello. Although he is considered one the world's greatest cellists, Ma is interested in other art forms in addition to the classical cello. Throughout his career, he has worked with artists and explored musical traditions from many parts of the world. In his website at www.yo-yoma.com, Ma writes, "Throughout my travels, I have thought about the culture, religions, and ideas that have been influential for centuries along the
(continued)

*Grammy Award:** A prize given in the United States every year to the best song, the best singer, and so on, in the music industry.

historic land . . . routes that made up the Silk Road and have wondered how these complex interconnections occurred and how new musical voices were formed from the **diversity** of these traditions." In 1998, Ma turned this dream of celebrating diverse cultures into a reality when he founded the Silk Road Project.

Yo-Yo Ma performs with two members of the Silk Road Ensemble at Carnegie Hall in New York.

Cross-cultural Exchange through the Silk Road Project

4   One way the Silk Road Project explores **cross-cultural** exchange among lands of the Silk Road and the West is through musical concerts. The project includes three types of music: traditional music of the Silk Road regions, Western classical music inspired by these cultures, and new music composed for the project. In 2002 Yo-Yo Ma and the Silk Road Ensemble released a CD called *Silk Road Journeys: When Strangers Meet*. In addition to musical concerts, the Silk Road Project has offered art exhibits, dance performances, films, and educational activities.

Planting the Seeds of Artistic and Cultural Growth

The CD *Silk Road Journeys*

5   The Silk Road Project has given opportunities to musicians and other artists to perform and **collaborate** within a **global** community. Furthermore, it has provided educational programs to promote the sharing of ideas and cultural traditions. Yo-Yo Ma explains, "Through this journey of discovery, the Silk Road Project hopes to plant the seeds of new artistic and cultural growth and to celebrate living traditions and musical voices throughout the world." Combining the history of the Silk Road, its traditional cultures, and new **contributions** by contemporary artists, the Silk Road Project has renewed the spirit of international exchange and global cooperation begun centuries ago by the ancient Silk Road traders.

Ma gives a master class in Seoul, South Korea.

Check Your Comprehension

Work with a partner and follow these steps.

1. On a piece of paper, write two questions for each paragraph in the article. Use question words such as *who, what, when, where, why,* and *how many.* On the back of the paper, write the answers to your questions.

2. Exchange questions with a partner. Answer the questions your partner wrote.

3. Check the answers your partner wrote for your questions. Are your partner's answers the same as the ones you wrote on the back of your paper?

4. Discuss the results. Which questions do you think were the most difficult? Why?

_____

_____

_____

_____

_____

Sharpen Your Vocabulary Skills

WORD PARTS

Suffixes

In the last chapter you learned that many English words are made up of several word parts: *prefixes, roots,* and *suffixes.*

> A **suffix** is a word part that is added to the end of a word. Suffixes usually indicate the function (noun, verb, adjective, or adverb) of a word in a sentence. Certain suffixes are used only for nouns, while others are used for verbs, adjectives, or adverbs. Learning suffixes will help you improve your vocabulary. Adding a suffix often involves a spelling change. If you are unsure about the spelling, check your dictionary.

Common Suffixes for Nouns

Suffix	Meaning	Examples
-ance (-ence)	*the act of doing something; the state of being something*	hesitance, confidence
-ion, -tion, -ation	*the act of doing something; the state or result of doing something*	revision, examination
-er, -or, -ian	*someone who does something*	teacher, sailor, politician
-ism	*a belief or set of ideas; the act of doing something*	Buddhism, criticism
-ist	*a person with a particular set of beliefs or with a knowledge of an area of study*	cyclist, pianist
-ment	*the act or result of doing something*	argument, development
-ness	*the state of being something*	sadness, softness
-ship	*the state of being something*	friendship, partnership
-ity	*the state of being something*	popularity, similarity
-ology	*the study or science of something*	anthropology, sociology

A. Add the correct suffix to the root word in each of the following sentences.

-er/-or   -ity   -ism

1. I was surprised at the (intense) _____ of his anger. [drop -e]

2. The new (conduct) _____ of the orchestra is excellent.

3. She is studying (journal) _____ at the University of Missouri.

-ist   -ship   -ness

4. She was filled with (sad) _____ when she heard the news.

5. She got her first job as a (journal) _____ at a small newspaper in Chicago.

6. I formed a (partner) _____ with my cousin.

-ence   -ion/-tion   -ment

7. There's an (elect) _____ for class president every fall.

8. I'm going to a (confer) _____ in Chicago for my job.

9. Our (govern) _____ is based on democracy.

-ism   -ment   -ology

10. Our economic system is based on (capital) _____.

11. (Meteor) _____ is the study of weather.

12. His (disappoint) _____ at not being chosen for the job was obvious.

-ness   -ion   -ity

13. I admire my grandmother's (kind) _____ and generosity.

14. Do you have an English (translate) _____ of this poem? [drop -e]

15. Can you believe my (stupid) _____? Once again, I locked my keys in the car.

B. Work with a partner. Look at the list of words from the articles "The Silk Road" and "Yo-Yo Ma and the Silk Road Project." Identify the suffix in each word and discuss how it changes the meaning of the word. Then think of other words with the same suffix. Finally, join another group and compare lists.

Word	Suffix	Change	Other Words
organization	-tion	The suffix *-tion* changes the verb *organize* to a noun.	circulation
similarity			
connection			
traveler			
imagination			
tourist			
civilization			
cellist			
diversity			
musician			
reality			
difference			

Sum It Up

Summarizing is a strategy that helps you see how well you have understood a reading passage. Look at the main idea sentences you wrote. Compare sentences with a partner. Then use the sentences to write a one-paragraph summary of "Yo-Yo Ma and the Silk Road Project."

_____

_____

_____

Share Your Thoughts

Work in small groups to discuss these questions.

1. Why do you think Yo-Yo Ma was attracted to the concept of the Silk Road as a theme for his music project?

2. In what ways is music a unifying force, bridging different cultures?

3. Is it possible to enjoy music sung in a language that you don't understand? How often do you usually listen to music of other cultures?

4. Do you think music can help increase appreciation of other cultures?

5. The Silk Road helped trade and the exchange of customs and ideas among Asia, the Middle East, and Europe. The Internet has been referred to as a modern Silk Road that encourages global cooperation. Discuss some positive and negative aspects of this global exchange of products, customs, and ideas.

Explore the Web

Use the Internet to do some research about the Silk Road Project. Find a list of musicians and artists who are part of the Silk Road Project. Work with a partner to choose one of the artists to read about. Find out what country the artist is from, what instrument he or she plays, and some interesting facts about the artist.

Go Beyond the Text

A. Work with a partner. Now that you have read about the Silk Road Project, discuss this question again: How do you think music can be a link between cultures?

B. Work with a group of three or four students to make a CD cover. Think of five songs you would include on your CD. Use the list to make and illustrate a CD cover. Think of a title for your CD and write it on the cover. Share your CD cover and list of songs with the class.

CHAPTER 3

Use Vocabulary Strategies

About the Artist

Dave Parker, one of the United Kingdom's top cartoonists, has been producing cartoons for over forty years. Parker has been a freelance cartoonist since 1954 and is a member of the Cartoonists Club of Great Britain. His cartoons have appeared in many newspapers including *The Daily Star, The Sun, The Oldie*, and *The Weekly News*. His work is also popular in Italy, where it appears regularly.

Look at the cartoon. It shows a man who works for a company that publishes a thesaurus, a type of dictionary in which words with similar meanings are grouped together. Discuss the cartoon with a partner and answer the questions.

1. What do you think the words *managing director, chief executive, administrator,* and *principal* mean? _____

   _____

2. What clues did you use to figure out the meanings?

   _____

   _____

3. Do you think the cartoon is funny? Why or why not?

   _____

   _____

> *When you used clues in the cartoon to guess the meaning of unfamiliar words, you were practicing an important vocabulary skill. Using clues will help you read more fluently.*

Sharpen Your Vocabulary Skills

English has the largest vocabulary of any language. Obviously, it would be impossible to memorize the definitions of all the words in an English dictionary. Luckily, you don't always need to know the exact definition of a word to understand the meaning of the sentence or paragraph in which it occurs. Like all good readers, you can develop strategies to help you determine the meanings of unfamiliar words. In this chapter you will learn some of these strategies.

Using Context to Guess Meaning

Do you know the meaning of the word *sagacious*? You might not know the exact meaning of this word, but when you come across it in a sentence, you may be able to guess its meaning. Read the following sentence and see if you can guess the meaning of *sagacious*.

- My grandfather is a <u>sagacious</u> man. He always makes good decisions, and I try to follow the advice he gives me.

What kind of person makes good decisions and gives good advice? Which of the following words would probably describe the writer's grandfather?

   a. foolish
   b. foreign
   c. wise

Using the **context** of *sagacious*—the words and sentences that come before and after it—should give you a general enough meaning to understand what the author is saying. One way good readers figure out the meaning of an unfamiliar word is to use clues from the word's context to help guess the meaning. Here are some strategies to help you guess the meaning of an unfamiliar word using its context.

Look for a definition of the word in the sentence. For example:

- The smallest unit of light is called a <u>photon</u>.

You don't need a dictionary to tell you what a *photon* is. The author gives you its meaning right in the sentence. Pay attention to punctuation because sometimes the meaning of a word is given in parentheses, between commas, or after a dash.

A. Circle the meanings of the underlined words in these sentences.

1. I think <u>etymology</u>, the study of the origin of words, is very interesting.

2. The idiom <u>*out of hand*</u> means impossible to control.

3. The three main groups of dinosaurs are <u>herbivores</u> (animals that eat plants), <u>carnivores</u> (animals that eat other animals), and <u>omnivores</u> (animals that eat plants and other animals).

Look for examples of the word in the sentence. Examples can help you figure out the general meaning of an unfamiliar word. Some expressions that introduce example clues are *such as, for instance, for example*, and *like*.

- The English language has lots of <u>homophones</u>, such as *two/too, bear/bare, him/hymn*, and *soar/sore*.

You might not know the exact definition of *homophone*, but from the examples in the sentence you can guess that homophones are words that sound alike but are spelled differently.

B. Use example clues to guess the meaning of the underlined word in each sentence. Circle the letter of the correct meaning.

1. My mother taught me how to be <u>frugal</u> when I didn't have much money. For example, she told me to use store coupons, buy things on sale, and cook my meals at home rather than eat at restaurants.
   a. thrifty
   b. kind
   c. helpful

2. The travel agent will show you a variety of <u>accommodations</u>, such as expensive hotels, moderately priced inns, and inexpensive youth hostels.

   a. places to visit
   b. ways to travel
   c. places to stay

3. When I make a sandwich I add lots of <u>condiments</u> like mustard, relish, mayonnaise, salt, pepper, and chopped onions.

   a. things you add to food so it will taste better
   b. types of sandwiches
   c. places to eat sandwiches

Look for a word or phrase in another part of the sentence that has a similar meaning to the word you don't know. Words such as *just as, too, and, similarly, like, as, also, related, resembling,* and *similar to* often signal similarity. For example,

- Barry was <u>astonished</u> when he won the lottery, and Warren was just as surprised.

You might not know the exact definition of *astonished*, but from the meaning of the sentence you can guess that it means something like *surprised*.

C. Look for words that signal similarity in each sentence to figure out the definition of the underlined word. Circle the best definition.

1. I am <u>bashful</u> in new situations. Similarly, my mother is shy when she meets new people.
   a. shy   **b.** smart   **c.** confused

2. We'll need to ask Dr. Havani for a scientific <u>perspective</u> on the problem. We should also call Dr. Lee for his point of view.
   a. science   **b.** viewpoint   **c.** problem

3. Her plan was <u>pragmatic</u>, and everyone in the room agreed that it was sensible and practical to proceed.
   a. sensible and practical   **b.** proceed   **c.** roomy

4. I was <u>reluctant</u> to try the spicy local food, and my husband was unwilling to taste it, too.
   a. tasty   **b.** spicy   **c.** unwilling

Look for a word or phrase in another part of the sentence that has the opposite meaning of the word you don't know. Words such as *but, however, in contrast, instead, even though, not,* and *although* indicate a contrast. For example:

• Jason was told to be respectful to his teachers; however, he is often <u>insolent</u>.

Even if you don't know the exact definition of *insolent,* from the meaning of the sentence you can guess that it is probably the opposite of *respectful.* What do you think *insolent* means?

    a. polite   (b.) rude   c. sweet

D. Look for words indicating a contrast in each sentence to figure out the meaning of the underlined word. Circle the letter of the correct meaning.

1. Although the members of the committee agree on all the major points of the plan, they are still spending too much time <u>quibbling over</u> the details.
   a. arguing about   **b.** paying for   **c.** ignoring

2. Even though some newscasters have praised the candidate for president, others have <u>maligned</u> him.
   a. honored   **b.** criticized   **c.** worked with

3. She grew up in a poor neighborhood in the city, but now she lives in an <u>affluent</u> suburb.
   a. wealthy   **b.** new   **c.** distant

Use a general sense of the sentence to make conclusions about the word and limit the possible meanings. For example:

• Everyone loves the way Pam dresses. She has <u>impeccable</u> taste in clothes. Her outfits always look just right.

Since the author said that people love the way Pam dresses, do you think *impeccable* has a positive or a negative meaning? Once you realize that impeccable has a positive meaning, you have limited the number of possible meanings for the word. Since you also know that her outfits always look just right, what do you think *impeccable* means?

    a. terrible   (b.) perfect   c. old

E. Read each sentence to make conclusions and limit the possible meanings of the underlined word. Circle the letter of the best meaning.

1. No one really understands how the magician made the rabbit disappear. His trick remains an <u>enigma</u>.
   a. cause   **b.** mystery   **c.** a kind of animal

2. I completely forgot to feed my cat yesterday, so when I fed her this morning she <u>devoured</u> the whole bowl of food in a few minutes.
      a. completely forgot   **b.** ate quickly   **c.** fed

3. Mr. Jefferson was the manager of the bank for several years. He began making mistakes several months ago and now he's been <u>relegated</u> to the position of assistant manager.
      a. moved to a less   **b.** fired from a job   **c.** given more money
          important position

When you come across an unfamiliar word in your reading, it is not always necessary to stop reading and look in a dictionary for an exact definition. First try to use clues in the sentence to help you figure out the meaning. Also train yourself to be satisfied with a general meaning of a word.

Be an Active Reader

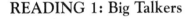

READING 1: Big Talkers

BEFORE YOU READ

Activate Your Background Knowledge

A. Read the statements in the chart. Do you agree or disagree with these statements? Check your response in the Before You Read columns.

Before You Read		Evaluate the Statements	After You Read	
Agree	Disagree	Statements	Agree	Disagree
		Elephants have the ability to make and hear sounds that humans cannot hear.		
		Only humans can communicate complex information to each other.		
		Elephants can communicate many types of messages over long distances.		
		We have a responsibility to help save animals that face extinction.		

B. Work with a partner. Discuss the statements in the chart in Exercise A and compare your responses.

Preview and Predict

C. Read the title and subtitle of the article on pages 55–57. Look at the picture and read the caption. Look at the headings. Can you guess what the article will be about? Think of three topics that might be discussed in the article and write them on the lines.

1. _____

2. _____

3. _____

Preview the Vocabulary

D. The words and phrases in the box are boldfaced in the article. Complete the Vocabulary Chart with words from the box. If necessary, use your dictionary.

> **Words to Watch**
>
> habitat   satellite dish   mate
> maintain   tusks   conservationist
> extinction   persuade

Vocabulary Chart	
Word	**Definition**
	a large circular piece of metal that receives the signals for radios and television
	two very long teeth that stick out of an animal's mouth
	to keep something in good condition by taking care of it
	to have sex to produce babies
	a person who is concerned about the protection of natural things such as wild animals or places
	the natural environment in which a plant or animal lives
	the state of no longer existing, such as for types of animals
	to make someone decide to do something by giving good reasons

You are going to read an article about how elephants communicate with each other. Write two questions you would like the article to answer.

1. _____

2. _____

AS YOU READ

As you read the article, think about the underlined words and phrases. Use context clues to guess the meaning of each word and write it in the space provided. Think about the strategies (definitions, examples, similarity signals, contrast, or general sense of sentence) that helped you figure out the meaning of the word.

Big Talkers

Earth's largest land animals have a lot to say—even when they don't seem to be making a sound.

These elephants are communicating with one another.

plod: _____

looking forward to: _____

calves: _____

1   Thirsty and hot, twelve elephants <u>plod</u> across the hot and dry African landscape. The water hole is less than a mile away now, and everyone in the group is <u>looking forward to</u> a good, long drink. Tired <u>calves</u>—baby elephants—want to stop, but mothers and aunts gently push them along. The older animals make soft, soothing noises. "We're almost there," they seem to say. "Just keep walking a little longer."

2   Suddenly everyone stops. Huge ears stretch out like **satellite dishes.** After a minute or two of what seems like silence, the animals turn and quickly walk away from the water hole. As they go, the adults stay close to the calves. So what happened? Why did the elephants change their <u>course</u>? They seemed to be listening to something. And whatever it was, they got the message to <u>flee</u>! Yet human ears were unable to hear the sounds. Elephants make lots of sounds that humans can hear, such as barks, snorts, roars, and trumpetlike calls. Often a group of elephants use such sounds to talk with other elephants.

(continued)

course: _____

flee: _____

Second Language

3   For years, scientists were <u>puzzled</u> by this type of elephant behavior, but now they have solved the mystery. They discovered that elephants have a "secret language" they use for communicating over long distances.

4   This special talk is based on <u>infrasound</u>, sounds so low that humans can't hear them. But elephants can hear them. The sounds can travel for several miles, allowing the six-ton animals to communicate across grasslands and forests in Africa or Asia.

5   Studying infrasound helps scientists understand elephant behavior. For example, the elephants heading to the water hole may have heard warning calls from another group of elephants. Perhaps those elephants saw a lion <u>slurping</u> water at the water hole. The lion looked hungry. The lion could not kill an adult elephant, but it might kill a calf. No drink would be worth that risk, so the herd turned away.

puzzled: _____

infrasound: _____

slurping: _____

Long-Distance Calls

6   Elephants use infrasound to communicate many types of messages over long distances. Some of their talk helps hold families

together. To understand how this works, you need to know a little about elephant families.

7   Female elephants spend their lives with mothers, sisters, and children. They live in close social groups called <u>herds</u>. A herd usually has ten to twenty members. The oldest female elephant in the herd—the <u>matriarch</u>—is the leader. She's in charge. Males live with their mother's herd until they are teenagers. Then they leave the herd and live alone.

8   The members of a herd often go off in different directions over large areas to look for food for their big <u>appetites</u>. (An adult elephant can eat 300 pounds of grass and plants in a single day!) Long-distance calls let

herds: _____

matriarch: _____

appetite: _____

elephants know where their relatives are. And when the matriarch says, "Come here!" the herd gathers within minutes.

9   Like curious kittens, elephant calves sometimes walk off and get into trouble. When that happens, they cry for help. Mothers respond with infrasound calls and other noises. Sisters and aunts answer the cries, too. "It's OK. Be careful. We're coming to help you."

10   Adult males and females often live far apart, so they use infrasound to find each other at mating time. Females **mate** only once every four years or so. When a female is

ready, she makes a special series of calls. Males who hear the calls <u>storm</u> toward her. Sometimes two or more males battle fiercely for a chance to mate with the female.

Hearing Aids

11   Elephants have several ways of learning what's going on around them. Elephants listen to sounds and communication calls with their large, powerful ears. An African elephant's ear can grow to be six feet long and four feet wide. When trying to hear something, the animal turns toward the sound and opens its ears wide.

12   At the same time, the elephant may raise its trunk to <u>sniff</u> at the wind. Elephants have an excellent sense of smell. <u>Odors</u> may help them figure out what they're hearing.

13   Elephants may have another way of learning what's going on around them. Although scientists haven't proved it, they have a <u>theory</u>. Some scientists think elephants can actually feel infrasound as certain sound waves travel through the ground.

```
storm:  _____

sniff:  _____

odors:  _____

theory: _____
```

Call for Help

14   Communication skills help Earth's largest land animals survive in the wild. But even these skills can't save elephants from **extinction**.

15   In 1997 Africa's elephant population was about 500,000. That may sound like a lot, but there were 1.3 million African elephants in 1979. More than half of the elephant population disappeared in only eighteen years.

16   How did this happen? First of all, people killed many elephants for their ivory **tusks** because ivory can be sold for a lot of money. But that's not the whole story. As the human population grew, people needed more land to live and grow crops on. Large areas of elephant **habitat** were wiped out in order to build farms and towns. Elephants from these areas <u>wandered into</u> human settlements. When they were hungry, the elephants ate valuable <u>crops</u> that farmers had planted. Some farmers became angry enough to kill the elephants.

```
wandered into: _____

crops: _____
```

How Will We Answer?

17   **Conservationists** are working hard to save elephants. They are trying to **persuade** people around the world to stop buying ivory. They believe all trade in ivory should be illegal. Elephant supporters are also working with African communities to **maintain** parks where elephants can be safe and will not harm crops. Some conservationists hope that tourists will visit these beloved animals there. That would mean jobs for local people, who would then view elephants as valuable animals that need to be protected.

AFTER YOU READ

Check Your Comprehension

A. True or false? Write T (True) or F (False) next to each of the following statements. If a statement is false, rewrite it to make it true.

_____ **1.** Humans can hear all the sounds elephants make.

_____ **2.** Scientists study infrasound to learn about elephant behavior.

_____ **3.** Male elephants live in close social groups called herds.

_____ **4.** Elephants have more than one way of learning what's going on around them.

_____ **5.** Elephants have a poor sense of smell.

_____ **6.** The number of elephants in the world is rapidly decreasing.

_____ **7.** There are several reasons why elephants face extinction.

Use Context Clues

B. Work with a partner and follow the steps.

1. Write both your definition and your partner's in the chart. Talk about the clues and strategy you used to come up with your definitions.

2. Look up the word or phrase in a dictionary and write the dictionary definition.

3. How close was your guess to the dictionary definition? Do you think your strategy was successful? Circle Yes or No in the last column.

Word/ Phrase	Your Definition	Your Partner's Definition	Dictionary Definition	Yes/No
plod				Yes No
looking forward to				Yes No
calves				Yes No
course				Yes No
flee				Yes No
puzzled				Yes No
infrasound				Yes No

Word/Phrase	Your Definition	Your Partner's Definition	Dictionary Definition	Yes/No
slurping				Yes No
herds				Yes No
matriarch				Yes No
appetite				Yes No
storm				Yes No
sniff				Yes No
odors				Yes No
theory				Yes No
wandered into				Yes No
crops				Yes No

Test Your Vocabulary

C. Complete each of the sentences that follow with the best word from the box. Be sure to use the correct form of the word.

habitat	satellite dish	mate
maintain	tusks	conservationist
extinction	persuade	

1. Her necklace was carved out of ivory from an elephant's _____.

2. When forests are cut down, many animals lose their _____.

3. Female elephants _____ only about every four years.

4. When the number of animals in a certain species gets very low, it faces _____.

5. My mother is a _____ who is trying to save beaches from being destroyed.

(continued)

6. We have a _____ on the roof of our house so that we can get a better picture on our television.

7. My parents finally _____ me to apply for the job.

8. It takes a lot of time to _____ a big garden.

Evaluate Your Ideas

1. Now that you have read the article, reread the statements in the Evaluate the Statements chart on page 53 and mark Agree or Disagree for each one in the After You Read columns.

2. Talk with a partner about why any of your new responses differed from the ones you made before you read the article.

3. Find and discuss the specific information in the article that supports each of your opinions.

Sum It Up

Write a one-paragraph summary of "Big Talkers." Remember to include only main ideas from the article in your summary.

_____

_____

_____

READING 2: Koalas

BEFORE YOU READ

You have just read an article about elephants in Africa. Now you are going to read an article about koalas in Australia. Like elephants, koalas are also threatened by extinction.

Preview and Predict

A. Preview the article on pages 62–63. Remember to look at the title, subtitle, headings, and pictures. Then make some predictions about the article and write them down.

1. _____

2. _____

3. _____

B. The words and phrases in the box are boldfaced in the article. Complete the Vocabulary Chart with words from the box. If necessary, use your dictionary.

Words to Watch

rage	hang on	pouch
bacteria	intestine	estimate
nutritious		

Vocabulary Chart

Word	Definition
	a pocket of skin that some animals keep their babies in
	containing many of the substances needed for bodies to stay healthy and grow
	the long tube that takes food from your stomach out of your body
	to continue happening with great force or violence
	to continue doing something even when it is difficult; to hold something tightly
	to judge the value or size of something
	very small living things, found everywhere, some of which can cause infection or disease

---

Set a Purpose

Complete the first two columns of the KWL Chart on the next page before you read the article. Write what you know about koalas in the first column. Write questions you would like to have answered in the second column.

KWL Chart		
What I Know (K)	What I Want to Know (W)	What I Learned (L)

AS YOU READ

As you read the article, pay attention to the underlined words. On a piece of paper or in your notebook, make a word definition chart similar to the one on page 54. Use context clues to write a definition for each underlined word.

Koalas
Can They Survive?

Disappearing Forests Threaten Koalas

1   Millions of koalas once lived in Australia. About 100,000 <u>survive</u> today. What's happening to these popular animals? Wildfires **raged** in Australia during January 2002. Firefighters struggled against them, but the <u>blazes</u> destroyed 600,000 acres of forest. The flames' victims included countless koalas. These tree-climbing mammals live only in eastern Australia. But the fire alarms caught the attention of koala lovers around the world. The wildfires were just part of a much larger problem: Forests are <u>vanishing</u> throughout eastern Australia. Cute and popular as koalas are, they're having trouble **hanging on**.

Picky Eaters with Big Appetites Need Lots of Food

2   Koalas' problems stem from being <u>picky eaters</u>. They like to eat only one thing—

<u>eucalyptus</u>, an Australian tree. Koalas use their big noses to sniff out tasty eucalyptus leaves. "If you offered them something else," says zookeeper Jennifer Moll, "they wouldn't know what to do with it. They'd starve before they'd eat a carrot."

For thousands of years, koalas' devotion to eucalyptus trees was actually a good choice. Eucalyptuses were once the most common trees in Australia. Their leaves contain <u>toxins</u>, or poisons, so few other animals eat eucalyptus. That means more food for koalas. Their stomachs have adapted to

Forest fires threaten koalas.

remove the toxins. Blood carries the toxins to a koala's <u>liver</u>, an organ that removes the poison.

3   Koalas weigh only 20 pounds. But they <u>gobble</u> almost 3 pounds of food a day. That's like a 60-pound child eating 9 pounds of food a day! Eucalyptus leaves aren't very **nutritious**, so koalas need huge servings to get enough energy. **Bacteria** in the koala's **intestines** turn the tough leaves into useful chemicals. Because they need so much food, koalas need lots of room. A single animal's home range, or <u>territory</u>, often covers several acres. If eucalyptus trees are rare, though, a koala may need dozens of acres to find its meals.

Home Is a Piece of a Puzzle

4   Even eating as much as they do, koalas don't have much energy. So they rest about 20 hours a day. That doesn't leave them much time to search for mates. For the population to multiply, koalas must be part of a <u>colony</u>, or group. Within a colony, the animals' home ranges fit together like pieces of a puzzle. Koalas generally live alone, but colony members form small groups at mating time. Five or so weeks after mating, koala mothers give birth. Each mother has a single <u>joey</u>, or baby. Blind and hairless, joeys are no bigger than jellybeans. Like other <u>marsupials</u>, such as kangaroos, koalas keep their joeys in **pouches**. After six months, joeys are strong enough to crawl out of their mothers' pouches. But they don't go off on their own until they're about a year old. Then it's time for the young koala to find its own "puzzle piece" to call home. But what happens when the puzzle starts to lose pieces?

Lost Puzzle Pieces Cause Problems

5   Like koalas, humans live in eastern Australia, too. Also like koalas, people need room—for houses, farms, parking lots, and so forth. To get space, Australians cut down trees. Humans have destroyed 80 percent of the forests where koalas once lived. Imagine having only 20 pieces of a 100-piece puzzle. It wouldn't be a pretty picture. Now imagine a male koala trying to find a female whose home range is on the other side of a highway. Or imagine a koala losing half its food supply to a parking lot. Like those stray puzzle pieces, the remaining bits of eucalyptus forest are scattered. That makes it much harder for koalas to gather during mating season. And there's nowhere to go if food runs out— or a fire starts. As a result, the koala population has <u>plunged</u>. The Australian Koala Foundation (AKF) **estimates** that there were 10 million koalas before 1788. That's when Europeans began moving to Australia. No one knows exactly how many koalas survive today. The AKF counts about 100,000. Other experts believe only about 40,000 remain.

What Happens Next?

6   What does the future hold for koalas? Can humans find ways to help them hold on? Australians hope so. "The koala," an Australian once said, "is essential to how we see ourselves." To protect koalas, Australia has created <u>reserves</u>, or safe places. Wildlife workers have also moved some koalas to less crowded areas. New colonies have formed—an encouraging sign. Saving koalas is possible. But it will take time, work, hard choices—and plenty of eucalyptus leaves.

AFTER YOU READ

Complete the KWL Chart

A. Fill in the third column in the KWL Chart on page 62. Write down information that you learned from reading the article. Did the article answer any of your questions from the second column? Which ones? Look at the things you wrote in the first column. Were any of your ideas confirmed or rejected in the article? Which ones?

B. In small groups, use your KWL Charts to discuss what you learned from the article.

Check Your Comprehension

C. Work with a partner and follow the steps.

1. On a separate piece of paper, write two questions for each paragraph in the article. Use question words such as *who, what, when, where, why,* and *how many*. On the back of the paper, write the answers to your questions.

2. Exchange questions with a partner. Answer the questions your partner wrote.

3. Check the answers your partner wrote for your questions. Are your partner's answers the same as the ones you wrote on the back of your paper?

Share Your Thoughts

Work in small groups to discuss these questions.

Are there any endangered animals in your country? What is being done to help save them?

Explore the Web

Endangered animals are species that are in danger of becoming extinct. Use the Internet to find out what animals are endangered. Choose an endangered animal and do some research on it. Use a search engine such as Google. Type in key words such as *endangered animals*.

Go Beyond the Text

1. Use the information you learned in the previous activity to complete the chart.

Name of endangered animal: _____

Location of animal: _____

Reasons the animal is endangered:

_____

_____

_____

_____

What is being done to save the animal:

_____

_____

_____

_____

2. Prepare an oral report about the animal you chose. Use the information in your chart. Find or draw a picture of the animal to show your classmates when you give your report.

CHAPTER 4

Understand Supporting Details

House on Main Street by St. George Tucker Aufranc

About the Artist

St. George Tucker Aufranc was born in 1943 in Staunton, Virginia. His mother was an art professor, but it wasn't until he was in his fifties that Aufranc, a medical doctor, gave much thought to art. In 1994, a friend encouraged him to try painting, and he found he liked it. Now Aufranc spends much of his free time drawing and painting, preferring to do landscapes and seascapes. He has shown his works at several galleries in the Boston area, and his works have also been shown and sold for fundraisers at the Museum of Fine Arts, Boston.

Look at the picture by Tucker Aufranc. Work with a partner. Discuss what you see and then answer the questions.

1. What is the picture about? What is the main idea?

   _____

2. What details does the artist include to show you that the house is abandoned? Make a list of the supporting details. Then compare lists with another pair of partners.

   _____   _____

   _____   _____

   _____   _____

   _____   _____

> *When you looked at the drawing, the supporting details helped you understand that the house was abandoned. In the same way, you should look for the supporting details as well as the main idea when you read. Knowing the main idea and some details will help you understand and remember what you read.*

Sharpen Your Reading Skills

IDENTIFYING SUPPORTING DETAILS

In Chapter 2 you learned that the main idea of a paragraph is the author's most important point about the topic. Once you have identified the main idea, you need to look for how the author supports, explains, or proves the main idea. Most of the sentences in a paragraph support the main idea by telling how, what, when, where, why, how much, or how many. These sentences are called supporting sentences; they provide examples, facts, descriptions, explanations, or reasons.

To identify supporting details, follow these steps:

1. **Ask yourself the question "What additional information does the author provide to help me understand the main idea?"** The answer to this question will help you find the supporting details.

2. **Look for signal words.** Sometimes signal words can help you identify supporting details. Supporting details are often introduced by signal words such as *first, second, next, also, in addition,* and *moreover*. Signal words are used to indicate that a supporting detail will follow.

Understanding the relationship between the main idea and the supporting details will improve your reading comprehension.

A. One sentence in each of the following groups is the main idea. The other two are supporting details. Write MI in front of the main idea and SD in front of the supporting details. Remember that supporting details are not as general as main ideas.

> **Example**
>
> _SD_ The American alligator is a species that lives in the southern United States.
>
> _MI_ There are two species of the large, powerful reptiles called alligators.
>
> _SD_ The smaller Chinese alligator makes its home in the Yangtze River.

1. _____ The type of clothing people wear depends on several things.

   _____ Climate and lifestyle help determine what people wear.

   _____ Popular fashion styles influence the kind of clothes people buy and wear.

2. _____ Jazz, including blues, ragtime, and swing, became popular in the early 1900s.

   _____ Many different types of music have developed in the past 100 years.

   _____ Electronic music is one of the latest trends in music.

3. _____ An abbreviation is a shortened form of a word or phrase.

   _____ Sometimes, an abbreviation is made from the first and last letter of a word, such as _Dr._ for "doctor."

   _____ Other times, the beginning of a word is used such as _Nov._ for "November."

4. _____ Carnivores, such as lions and dogs, have sharp teeth for grabbing their prey and tearing its flesh.

   _____ Herbivores, like cows and horses, have broad grinding teeth for eating plants.

   _____ Mammals, which eat a wide variety of foods, have developed special kinds of teeth to suit their needs.

5. _____ One of the oldest newspapers in the world is _The Times_, which is printed in London, England.

   _____ _The Times_ was started by John Walter in 1785.

   _____ The paper was first called the _Universal Daily Register_, but the name was changed to _The Times_ in 1788.

B. Read each topic sentence. Then check the facts from the list that follows that would support the main idea.

Example

The Internet provides a format for a huge range of activities.

✓ **a.** Thousands of companies have websites where customers can see, order, and pay for products.

✓ **b.** Radio stations can play their programs over the Internet.

___ **c.** The first e-mail was sent in 1971.

✓ **d.** Millions of people send and receive messages by e-mail every day.

✓ **e.** Museums can display their exhibits on the Internet.

---

1. **With their special adaptations, camels are ideally suited to carry heavy loads across dry, hot, sandy deserts.**

   _____ **a.** They have padded feet that are able to grip well on sandy ground.

   _____ **b.** They are very strong and can carry up to 1,000 pounds.

   _____ **c.** There are two types of camels, the Dromendary or single-humped camel, and the two-humped or Bactrian camel.

   _____ **d.** Camels will eat almost anything including thorny shrubs and thistles that grow in the desert.

   _____ **e.** Camels are able to go for days without food as they live off of the fat stored in their humps.

   _____ **f.** They have slitlike nostrils that can be closed down tightly and heavy eyebrows and eyelashes to protect their eyes from sand.

   _____ **g.** Rugs, tents, and clothes are made from camel hair.

2. **Some insects, such as ants, bees, and termites, live in highly organized colonies, and members have specific jobs to perform.**

   _____ **a.** The queen's job is to mate and lay eggs.

   _____ **b.** The task of some members is to gather food.

   _____ **c.** Repairing and guarding the nest is the duty of other members.

   _____ **d.** Insects feed on a variety of both plants and animals.

(continued)

_____ e. Some insects in the colony take care of the queen and feed and care for the young.

_____ f. All insects have three body parts and three sets of legs.

_____ g. Still others, whose job is to defend the colony, grow large, with big heads and powerful jaws.

C. Read the following paragraphs and answer the questions that follow.

Example

    English dictionaries are full of information about words. For one thing, a dictionary tells you how to spell and pronounce each word correctly. It also tells you the meaning of each word. Since many words in English have more than one meaning, a dictionary gives all the meanings. In addition, a dictionary identifies the part of speech (noun, verb, adjective, and so on) of each word. Some dictionaries also include information about the etymology (origin and history) of the words.

a. What is the topic of the paragraph? Dictionaries

b. What is the main idea? Dictionaries are full of information about words.

c. What four details does the author give to support the main idea?

    1. A dictionary tells how to spell and pronounce words.

    2. A dictionary tells the meaning of a word.

    3. A dictionary gives all the meanings.

    4. A dictionary identifies the part of speech of the word.

1.   The Earth has a wide range of different climates. The two polar regions, the North Pole and the South Pole, are cold, snowy, and icy. Tropical areas, which are near the equator, are hot, humid, and wet. Located in between the polar and tropical areas are temperate regions, which have moderate rainfall, warm summers, and cool winters.

a. What is the topic of the paragraph? _____

b. What is the main idea? _____

c. What three facts does the author give to support the main idea?

    1. _____

    2. _____

    3. _____

2. If you have ever been to the sea, you have probably seen seaweed growing on rocks or along the shore. Did you know that seaweed has many important uses? Seaweed is rich in vitamins and minerals and is a popular food in many parts of the world. Seaweed is also used to make fertilizer. In addition, seaweed is useful because it provides homes and food for many sea animals. It might surprise you to learn that some types of seaweed are also used to make lipstick, soap, and even film for cameras!

a. What is the topic of the paragraph? _____

b. What is the main idea? _____

c. What four examples does the author give to support the main idea? _____

1. _____

2. _____

3. _____

4. _____

3. Meteorologists, people who study the weather, say that in recent years there has been an increase in extreme weather conditions all over the world. For example, 562 tornadoes hit the United States in May of 2003, setting a record for any month. Another record was set in Switzerland, which had the hottest June in 250 years. Australia also experienced extreme weather as it was hit by the longest drought ever. At the same time, a heat wave hit India. Temperatures rose to 113–120 degrees Fahrenheit (45–49 degrees Celsius). In Sri Lanka, a cyclone caused serious floods. It was also hotter than normal in France, England, and Wales, while China and much of Asia experienced more severe flooding than usual.

a. What is the topic of the paragraph? _____

b. What is the main idea? _____

c. How many examples does the author give to support the main idea? _____

4. Although I could have moved anywhere after I graduated from college, I chose New York City for several reasons. First of all, many of my friends were moving to New York and lots of others already lived there, so I knew I would have a good social life. New York also has lots of job opportunities in my field, finance, and I didn't think I'd have a hard time finding a job. I enjoy theater and living near Broadway was very attractive to me. It would be easy to get tickets and see lots of plays. Finally, I love clothes and shopping and New York is one of the fashion capitals of the world.

a. What is the topic of the paragraph? _____

b. What is the main idea? _____

c. How many reasons does the author give to support the main idea? _____

_____

> To help you understand the main idea of a text, the writer adds sentences that provide supporting details. The supporting details give more information about the topic. After you identify the main idea, you should look for details that support it. Ask yourself, **"What additional information does the author provide to help me understand the main idea?"**

Scanning for Details

Sometimes you want to find a specific detail or piece of information in a reading quickly. Usually, you know exactly what information you are looking for, and you concentrate on finding that particular answer.

> To find specific information, you should use a reading technique called **scanning**. When you scan, you read quickly to find the specific information you need. To scan, you move your eyes quickly across the text. You do not have to read every word.

To scan effectively you need to do several things.

1. Have a question in mind and know the specific kind of information you are looking for in order to answer it: a name, a date, a time, a key word.

2. Anticipate how the information you need will appear and use clues to help you find it quickly. For example, if you want to know when something happened, you would quickly read the passage looking only for a date. If you need to know who did something, you would scan for a name.

3. Use headings, boldfaced words, italics, numbers, charts, quotation marks, or any other aid that will help you identify the section that could contain the information you are looking for.

4. Ignore the words and information that aren't important for your purpose.

5. Move your eyes rapidly across the text until you find the information and then stop reading.

D. Scan the passage about advertising in the 1920s to answer the questions that follow.

Advertising became a big business in the United States in the 1920s. According to some statistics, the amount of money spent on advertising in the United States increased from about $200 million in 1880 to nearly $3 billion in 1920. By 1920 advertisers were spending about $15 annually on every man, woman, and child in the United States. That's a grand total of $2.8 billion! The advertising dollars were used to attract people to buy a flood of new products, including automobiles, radios, household appliances, and personal products. Almost as soon as a new product hit the market, advertisers tried to convince people that it was something they absolutely needed and must buy. Some advertisers even hired psychologists to help them understand the best ways to reach new customers. Others sold products by appealing to people's fears. For example, the makers of a mouthwash called Listerine used the scientific term *halitosis* (which means bad breath) to urge consumers to rush out to buy Listerine to avoid the embarrassment of halitosis. The ad campaign was so successful that Listerine sales went from $100,000 per year in 1921 to more than $4 million in 1927.

1. How much money was spent on advertising in the United States in 1880? _____

2. How much money was spent on advertising in the United States in 1920? _____

3. What does *halitosis* mean? _____

4. When did Listerine sales reach more than $4 million? _____

Be an Active Reader

READING 1: The Power of Advertising

BEFORE YOU READ

Activate Your Background Knowledge

A. You have probably seen many advertisements in your life. Think about what you already know about advertising. Reread the above paragraph about advertising in the 1920s. Try to remember some ads you have really liked and some ads you have found annoying. Complete the following sentences by choosing one of the words or phrases in parentheses, and then compare and discuss answers with a partner.

1. When I see an ad I like, I (usually, sometimes, rarely) buy the product.

2. I think most of the ads I see are (informative, entertaining, annoying).

(continued)

3. In my opinion, (too much, the right amount of, not enough) money is spent on advertising.

4. I think ads (are, are not) a reflection of society.

Preview and Predict

B. Read the title of the article on pages 76–78, and ask yourself, "In what ways can advertising be a powerful tool in society?" Look at the pictures of the ads and read the captions. Have you ever seen any of these ads? Have you ever bought or tried any of the products in the ads? Look at the headings of each section. Can you guess what the article will be about? Think of several topics that might be discussed in the article. Write the topics on the lines.

> **Example**
>
> How much money advertising costs _____

1. _____   3. _____

2. _____   4. _____

Preview the Vocabulary

C. The words and phrases in the box are boldfaced in the article. Complete the Vocabulary Chart with words from the box. If necessary, use your dictionary.

> **Words to Watch**
>
> | | | | |
> |---|---|---|---|
> | excessive | campaign | dominate | rival |
> | promote | contemporary | atmosphere | |
> | perseverance | materialism | temptation | |

Vocabulary Chart	
Word	**Definition**
	the belief that getting money and possessions is the most important thing in life
	the feeling that an event, situation, or place gives you
	belonging to the present time
	to help something develop and be successful
	determination to keep trying to do or achieve something
	to have power and control over someone or something
	a series of actions intended to achieve a particular result
	a person, group, or organization that you compete with
	much more than is reasonable or necessary
	a strong desire to have or do something, although it is wrong, bad, or silly, just because it seems attractive

Set a Purpose

You are going to read an article about advertising. What do you want to find out about this topic? Write two questions you would like the article to answer.

1. _____

2. _____

The author of this article supports the main idea of most paragraphs with examples. As you read the article, underline the main idea of each paragraph. Then circle two examples in the paragraph that support the main idea.

The Power of Advertising
The Cost of Advertising

1   Teams of writers, artists, and designers work together at advertising companies to produce effective ads. Although advertising campaigns can dramatically increase the sales of a product, the cost is not cheap. Billions of dollars are spent each year in advertising **campaigns** to market products. Newspaper ads can cost thousands of dollars, magazine and Web ads can cost hundreds of thousands of dollars, and television commercials can run into the millions. For example, a single commercial run on TV during the Super Bowl can cost $2.3 million. Why do companies spend so much money to **promote** their products or services? When successful, advertising can create powerful images connected to a particular brand. Whether we like them or not, ads become part of our consciousness and may remain in our memories for decades.

The Power of Slogans

2   With so many forms of communication competing for our attention today, it is not easy to get one message to stand out from the others. This is the challenge of advertising, to create slogans, or short memorable phrases, that will remind us of a particular brand. Although sometimes annoying when heard over and over again, catchy slogans become part of our consciousness. The repeated phrase "Can you hear me now?" in Verizon cell phone ads has become a standard phrase in popular culture. "Don't leave home without it," an American Express credit card slogan, is another phrase that is part of the collective American memory.

Creating a Warm Atmosphere

3   Some ads aim to create a feeling of warmth and comfort. "You're in good hands with Allstate" has been a successful slogan for an insurance company. "Reach out and touch someone," an AT&T slogan, showed the happiness that occurs when customers telephone family and friends. These ads created a feeling of close human interaction within a giant telecommunications company. "Fly the friendly skies of United" suggests an **atmosphere** of hospitality at this airline. The Pillsbury food company has shown scenes of mothers taking cookies or cakes out of the oven to promote their baking products. "Nothing says loving like something from the oven" is the slogan that associates their products with the warmth of family and home.

The Appeal of Humor

4   Other ads use humor to catch the attention of an audience. A popular ad campaign for Alka-Seltzer, a stomach indigestion medication, featured images of people overeating; for example,

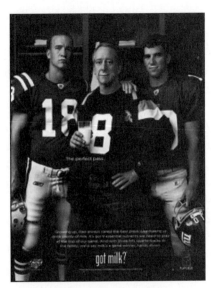

Professional football players Archie Manning (retired) and sons Peyton and Eli wear milk moustaches.

campaign that shows athletes exercising and pushing themselves to the limit. Nike's simple slogan "Just do it" encourages viewers to jump into some type of physical exercise themselves. Avis, the car rental company with sales less than the sales of their **rival** Hertz, ran a very successful campaign with the slogan "We're number two. We try harder." Such ads point to the benefits of persistence, creating a positive image for the company.

Nike's slogan is one of the most famous in advertising history.

one person had eaten an entire pizza, while another had just finished a huge dinner. Each actor sighed, "I can't believe I ate the whole thing!" Other ads aim for humorous images. A series of advertisements for milk called "Got Milk?" has featured famous celebrities with milk on their upper lips, looking as if they are wearing milk "moustaches." The Got Milk television commercials were created in 1993 for the National Dairy Council to help boost declining milk sales. More than 130 celebrities, including actors, models, and musicians, have worn a milk moustache in the ads. If the members of the audience smile when viewing an advertisement, they are more likely to have a positive attitude toward the product or message.

Trying Harder

5   Inspiration and **perseverance** are themes appearing in numerous ads. The sportswear company Nike has created a successful ad

The Annoyance Factor

6   Critics of advertising point out that audiences are subjected to a vast number of ads pushing them to buy, buy, buy. They say that the strong forces of advertising contribute to a consumer society that is based on **materialism**. Other people simply find ads annoying when they take up huge amounts of space in newspapers or magazines, interrupt television programs, or pop up on computer screens. Parents, in particular, often feel frustrated by **excessive** advertising and may try to train children to resist the **temptations** of ads. They find themselves having to tell their children that they do not really need to eat every new kind of snack food or buy every new toy on the market. It is estimated that advertisers spend more than $12 billion per year on advertising messages aimed at the

(continued)

youth market. Today, the average child watches more than 40,000 television commercials per year.

A Mirror of Contemporary Society

7   Most of us, however, will admit to occasionally finding at least some ads entertaining or even informative. Some people fondly remember advertisements from years ago. In fact, ads are viewed as a reflection of popular trends and social values of their era. Experts study past and present ads as a way of examining the attitudes and behavior of a particular culture. The noted Canadian scholar Marshall McLuhan observed: "Historians and archaeologists will one day discover that the ads of our time are the richest and most faithful reflections that any society ever made of its entire range of activities." Whether we find ads annoying or not, it is certain that they will continue to appear in much of what we read and watch. Advertising continues to **dominate** popular media, and it continues to reveal truths about **contemporary** society.

AFTER YOU READ

Check Your Comprehension

A.   True or false? Write T (True) or F (False) next to each of the following statements. If a statement is false, rewrite it to make it true.

_____   **1.** Most people like the ads they remember from years ago.

_____   **2.** It is very difficult for advertisers to get a message noticed.

_____   **3.** If you hear an advertisement often enough, it becomes part of your consciousness.

_____   **4.** Humor is the only method of catching the attention of an audience.

_____   **5.** Advertisements aimed at children frustrate some parents.

_____   **6.** Millions of dollars are spent annually to market products.

_____   **7.** Advertisers always like to create a sense of emotional well-being.

_____   **8.** Advertising can be thought of as a mirror of a society.

_____   **9.** Critics say that advertising contributes to creating a materialistic society.

_____   **10.** Most ads have themes of inspiration and perseverance.

_____   **11.** A "catchy" slogan is a slogan that grabs the attention of the audience.

Scan for Details

B. Scan the article to complete the chart and answer the questions as quickly as possible. Then compare answers with a partner.

Question	Question Word(s)	Type of Information	Answer
Who used "I can't believe I ate the whole thing!" as a slogan?	who	name	Alka-Seltzer
When were the Got Milk television commercials created?			
How much can a single TV commercial run during the Super Bowl cost?			
Who is a noted Canadian scholar?			
How many celebrities have worn a milk mustache in ads?			
What is a popular American Express slogan?			
How much money do advertisers spend on ads aimed at the youth market?			
How many commercials does the average child watch per year?			

Test Your Vocabulary

C. Complete each of the sentences that follow with the best word from the box. Be sure to use the correct form of the word.

excessive	campaign	dominate
promote	contemporary	atmosphere
perseverance	temptation	
materialism	rival	

1. My brother has hired an advertising agency to help him _____ his product.

2. The museum has a special exhibition of _____ Japanese prints.

3. Jeanine's husband worries about her _____ spending.

4. The company will announce its new advertising _____ next week.

5. The airline company lowered its fares so that it could compete with its _____.

6. My aunt is very nice, but she tends to _____ the conversation.

7. Jose shows great _____ in trying to improve his English.

8. Mai loves to buy things. Many people criticize her for her _____.

9. The _____ at their house has been much happier since he got his new job.

10. I really had to resist the _____ to hit him.

D. Use context clues to guess the meaning of the boldfaced words and phrases. Write a definition or synonym of the words and phrases. Then compare answers with a partner.

1. This is the challenge of advertising, to create **slogans**, or short memorable phrases, that will remind us of a particular brand.

   _____

2. Newspaper ads can cost thousands of dollars, magazine and Web ads can cost hundreds of thousands of dollars, and television commercials can **run into** the millions.

   _____

3. "Reach out and touch someone," an AT&T slogan, showed the happiness that occurs when customers telephone family and friends. These ads created a feeling of close human interaction within a **giant** telecommunications company.

_____

4. A popular ad campaign for Alka-Seltzer, a stomach indigestion medication, featured images of people **overeating**; for example, one person had eaten an entire pizza, while another had just finished a huge dinner.

_____

5. Critics of advertising **point out** that audiences are subjected to millions of ads pushing them to buy, buy, buy.

_____

Sum It Up

Write a one-paragraph summary of "The Power of Advertising." Remember to include only important ideas from the article in your summary.

_____

_____

_____

_____

Share Your Thoughts

A. Work in small groups to discuss these questions.

1. What kinds of ads do you think are the most effective? Why?

2. What are some TV commercials you like? Which ones do you dislike?

3. When you go shopping for food (or clothes, games, cars, technical equipment, and so on), do you buy products you have seen advertised on TV commercials? Why or why not? Explain your answer.

B. Choose one of the questions in Exercise A and write a paragraph about it.

_____

_____

_____

_____

_____

_____

READING 2: International Marketing *No Va*

BEFORE YOU READ

You have just read an article about the power of advertising. Now you are going to read an article about advertising and marketing products in different countries.

Activate Your Background Knowledge

A. Read the statements in the chart. Do you agree or disagree with these statements? Check your response in the first two columns. You will check the last columns after you read.

Before You Read		Evaluate the Statements	After You Read	
Agree	**Disagree**	**Statement**	**Agree**	**Disagree**
		All products can be marketed the same way in different cultures.		
		Advertising slogans can always be translated successfully from one language to another.		
		International marketing is more successful when it appeals to each culture's particular values.		

B. Work with a partner. Discuss the statements and compare responses.

Preview and Predict

C. Read the title and subtitle of the article on pages 84–86. Look at the headings. Read the first and last paragraph of the article. Can you guess what the article will be about? Think of several topics that might be discussed in the article. Write the topics on the lines.

1. _____

2. _____

3. _____

4. _____

Preview the Vocabulary

D. The words in the box are boldfaced in the article. Use context clues to guess the meaning of the boldfaced words in the exercise. Write definitions or synonyms of the words. If necessary, use your dictionary. Then compare answers with a partner.

Words to Watch

indicators	adaptations	shrinking	interpret
blunder	tricky	exaggeration	individualism
collectivism	slang	barrier	

1. Sometimes the cost of a product is an **indicator** of its quality. In fact, many people think that the more something costs, the better it is.

   _____

2. There were several **tricky** questions on the math test. It took me a long time to figure out the answers.

   _____

3. In some places forests are **shrinking**, while in other places deserts are getting bigger.

   _____

4. Some parts of the story were not appropriate for children, so I wrote an **adaptation** for a younger audience.

   _____

5. I made a terrible **blunder** when I called my professor by the wrong name. I hope he forgives me for my careless mistake.

   _____

(continued)

6. John said that over a 1,000 people came to his concert last night. I'm sure the number is an **exaggeration**. There were probably more like 200 people in the audience.

_____

7. In cultures where **individualism** is stressed, people believe in the value of personal success and independence.

_____

8. On the other hand, in cultures where **collectivism** is stressed, people believe in the family, cooperation, and the importance of the group.

_____

9. A chicken is a type of bird kept on a farm, but the word _chicken_ is also **slang** for someone who isn't very brave.

_____

10. Kim speaks Korean and Jose speaks Spanish. They are in the same English class and are becoming good friends despite their language **barrier**.

_____

11. We **interpreted** his silence to mean that he was guilty.

_____

Set a Purpose

You are going to read an article about international marketing. What do you want to find out about this topic? Write two questions you would like the article to answer.

1. _____

2. _____

AS YOU READ

International Marketing _No Va_
How to Recognize Cultural Differences and Sell a Product in a New Market

1 Your company is ready to take its new product to an international market. The product has sold well in Canada and there is a need for it in other countries. In addition, the economy is thriving. All the **indicators** are positive, so you use the same marketing campaign that worked in Canada. But you find that your early sales are much lower than you anticipated. Why? There are many possible reasons, but if history is any indication, one of the major failings of companies expanding to international

markets is how they market the product, no matter how good it is.

2   You can't help but smile at the story of Chevrolet marketing their brand new Nova in Latin America in the early 1970s and then not understanding why it didn't sell. The problem lay in the language. *No va* in Spanish means "doesn't go," which is exactly what happened to the sales figures. To be fair to Chevrolet, they were not alone in their international marketing **blunder**. Gerber baby food, Coke, Pepsi, Perdue poultry, and Gillette have all taken their turn as the subject of international marketing jokes.

3   With modern technology **shrinking** our world, international borders are becoming less of a **barrier** between people. The temptation is to believe that this shrinkage will emphasize our cultural similarities when in fact the opposite has been found to be true. As companies become more global, many countries have become more protective of their culture. This increased sense of patriotism makes successful entry of foreign consumer products more difficult and the need for marketing **adaptations** more important.

4   In his best-selling book *The Lexus and the Olive Tree*, Thomas Friedman quotes his friend Yaron Ezrahi's observation about globalization. Ezrahi said: "There are two ways to make a person feel homeless—one is to destroy his home and the other is to make his home look and feel like everybody else's home." The best way to avoid creating a feeling of homelessness is to understand the culture you are selling to and make consumers think that your product is unique to their needs. Before you can understand marketing

to new cultures, you must first understand what culture is. Culture can be defined as a set of values and beliefs that are learned, shared, and passed on to give us our identity. With that definition in mind, several cultural issues must be considered when marketing across cultures.

Be Careful When You Translate

5   Language is the most obvious concern you must think about when marketing across cultures. Translating the names of products and company names can be **tricky**. And you must be very careful when translating advertising slogans. When you decide to translate your company slogan or the name of the product, make sure that there are no **slang** expressions, which can lead to embarrassment. A notable and humorous example was the Chinese translation of Pepsi's slogan "Come alive with the Pepsi Generation," which translated to "Pepsi brings your ancestors back from the grave." This may have been good for sales, but I don't think Pepsi could actually do that.

Know the Meanings of Colors, Numbers, and Symbols

6   In different cultures, colors, numbers, and symbols have very different meanings. Know what the color of mourning is and don't advertise cars in that color. Learn what numbers are unlucky and avoid packaging items in those units. Understand which symbols do not transfer across cultures and then do not use them. For example, the thumbs-up sign may be a pleasant one in the United States, but Australians will **interpret** it very differently.

(continued)

Consider Traditional Values

7   Cultures vary considerably in what they consider to be traditional values. For example, in Germany there is a tradition of excellence in engineering, in England, many people dislike **exaggeration**, and the Chinese have a tradition of valuing old, wise, and consistent over new, aggressive, and improved. These traditions are only a few examples of the ones that must be known and considered for successful marketing.

Think about Individualism versus Collectivism

8   Another difference between cultures that should be considered is the importance placed on **individualism** versus **collectivism**. In the United States and Canada, individualism is very important. Many people in these countries believe in the value of personal success, independence, and the concept of "pulling yourself up by the boot straps" (solving a problem yourself without outside help). On the other hand, in collectivist cultures such as Japan, China, and Mexico, people believe in the family, cooperation, and the importance of the group. It is important to know whether the culture you are advertising to is individualistic or collectivistic; many mistakes can be made in not knowing. The central principle of marketing across cultures is no different from marketing within a single culture—know your market! The challenge is that it is easier to know about the culture you live in than one you are just visiting.

9   The most important thing is to know that there are cultural differences and to address them. Not all cultures are the same, and they don't want to be. Any effort to understand the differences will be well received and your balance sheet will provide you with proof.

AFTER YOU READ

Check Your Comprehension

A.   Circle the letter of the word or phrase that correctly completes each statement or answers the question.

1. The author believes that the successful entry of foreign products into a market is made more difficult because _____.
    a. many countries have become more protective of their culture
    b. cultural similarities are prevalent
    c. the quality of the products is poor

2. The term *culture* is defined in the _____.
    a. first paragraph
    b. fourth paragraph
    c. last paragraph

3. Gerber baby food, Coke, Pepsi, Perdue poultry, and Gillette are used as examples of companies that _____.
   a. have made a lot of money
   b. sell excellent products
   c. have made marketing blunders

4. According to the author, as our world is shrinking, many countries are becoming _____.
   a. more protective of their culture
   b. less patriotic
   c. more individualistic

5. The thumbs-up sign is used as an example of _____.
   a. an unlucky number
   b. a creative slogan
   c. a symbol that does not translate across cultures

6. Which culture has a tradition of valuing old, wise, and consistent over new, aggressive, and improved?
   a. Chinese
   b. Canadian
   c. German

7. The differences between individualistic and collectivist cultures are

   _____.
   a. slightly significant
   b. very significant
   c. not significant

8. The author believes that the principle "know your market" is

   _____.
   a. important both to marketing across cultures and within a single culture
   b. a collectivist point of view
   c. unimportant in today's shrinking world

Sharpen Your Vocabulary Skills

WORD PARTS

You have learned that suffixes usually indicate the function (noun, verb, adjective, or adverb) of a word in a sentence. Study the chart of common suffixes that are used to make adjectives.

	Adjective Suffixes	
Suffix	**Meaning**	**Examples**
-able, -ible	*capable of; having a particular quality*	manageable, comfortable, responsible
-ful	*full of*	beautiful, harmful
-en	*made of something; to make something have a particular quality*	wooden, golden
-ic, -ical	*of; like; relating to a particular thing*	economic, economical
-less	*without something*	childless, careless, endless
-ous, -ious	*having, full of*	dangerous, furious
-y	*full of or covered with something; tending to do something*	hairy, curly, sleepy
-ive	*having a particular quality*	creative, descriptive

Work with a partner. Look at the chart of words from the article "International Marketing *No Va*." Identify the suffix in each word and write down how it changes the meaning of the word. Then think of other words with the same suffix. Finally, join another pair and compare lists.

Word	Suffix	Change	Other Words
protective	-ive	Changes the verb protect to an adjective	creative
successful			
political			
homeless			
notable			
humorous			
pushy			
individualistic			
aggressive			

Pronoun Reference

Pronouns (such as *he, she, they, his, hers, their, it, who, this, that, these, those, one,* and *ones*) are small but important words that replace nouns. Writers often use pronouns to avoid repeating the same nouns over and over. Good readers look for pronouns and identify the nouns they refer to. The ability to identify pronoun referents, or antecedents, will help you read faster and understand more.

A. Read the paragraph from the article. Notice the underlined pronoun *they* in several sentences. Each time it refers to a different noun. Look for the noun that each *they* replaces and circle it.

Critics of advertising point out that audiences are subjected to a vast outpouring of ads pushing them to buy, buy, buy. They say that the seemingly relentless forces of advertising contribute to a consumer society that is based on materialism. Other people simply find ads annoying when they take up huge amounts of space in newspapers or magazines, interrupt television programs, or pop up on computer screens. Parents, in particular, often feel frustrated by excessive advertising and may try to train their children to resist the temptations of ads. They find themselves having to tell their children that they do not really need to eat every new kind of snack food or buy every new toy on the market.

B. Read the following sentences from the articles in this chapter. Notice each underlined pronoun and look for the noun(s) it refers to.

1. Not all cultures are the same, and they don't want to be.

   they = _____

2. The most important thing is to know that there are cultural differences and to address them.

   them = _____

3. A series of advertisements for milk has featured famous celebrities with milk on <u>their</u> upper lips, looking as if they are wearing milk "moustaches."

   their = _____

4. The best way to avoid creating a feeling of homelessness is to understand the culture you are selling to and make consumers think that your product is unique to <u>their</u> needs.

   their = _____

5. The product has sold well in Canada and there is a need for <u>it</u> in other countries.

   it = _____

6. For example, the thumbs-up sign may be a pleasant <u>one</u> in the United States, but Australians will interpret it very differently.

   one = _____

Evaluate Your Ideas

1. Now that you have read the article, reread the statements in the Evaluate the Statements Chart on page 82 and mark Agree or Disagree for each one in the After You Read column.

2. Talk to a partner about why any of your new responses differed from the ones made before you read the article.

3. Find and discuss the specific information in the article that supports each of your opinions.

Sum It Up

Summarizing orally will help you remember the important information in your reading. Work in small groups. Imagine that your friend asked you to explain the article you just read, "International Marketing *No Va*." First make a list of the main points in the article. Then use the list to explain what the reading was about in your own words. Take turns explaining the article to the other members of your group.

Share Your Thoughts

Work in small groups to discuss these questions.

1. Is your culture more individualistic or collectivistic? Give some specific examples to support your opinion.

2. What are some of the most important traditional values in your culture? How are these values reflected in the way products are marketed in your country?

3. Discuss the meanings of specific colors, numbers, and symbols in your culture. How can they have an impact on advertising?

4. The author refers to this quote: "There are two ways to make a person feel homeless—one is to destroy his home and the other is to make his home look and feel like everybody else's home." Do you agree with this idea? Why or why not? What other ways can you think of to make a person feel homeless?

5. What do you think are the most important things companies should consider when they market their products in other countries?

Explore the Web

Work with a partner. Use the Internet to find the information you need to match the slogans in the left column with their with brands in the right column.

_____ 1. *Good to the last drop*   **a.** Volkswagen

_____ 2. *Breakfast of Champions*   **b.** Pepsi

_____ 3. *Drivers wanted*   **c.** Coca-Cola

_____ 4. *Diamonds are forever*   **d.** Wheaties cereal

_____ 5. *It's the Cola*   **e.** Maxwell House Coffee

_____ 6. *It's the real thing*   **f.** De Beers diamonds

Go Beyond the Text

1. Think of an advertising slogan that is famous in your country. If possible, bring in a print ad in your language. Translate the slogan for your classmates and discuss whether it would be effective in English and for an American audience.

2. Work with a group of three or four students. Think of a product you want to sell. Plan and act out a TV commercial for your product. Write your own original slogan in the box.

```



```

CHAPTER 5

Analyze the Text

Sunflowers by Vincent van Gogh

About the Artist

Vincent van Gogh was born in the Netherlands in 1853. He was self-taught as an artist. His first works showed the lives of farmworkers and the poor. In 1886 Van Gogh moved to Paris to live with his brother, Theo, an art dealer who introduced him to the famous painters of his time. In 1888 he moved to Arles, in the south of France, and was immediately struck by the bright colors of the Mediterranean. *Sunflowers* was one of the paintings Van Gogh painted in the south of France.

Look at Van Gogh's painting and discuss it with a partner. Then answer the questions.

1. What is the painting about?

   _____

2. How are the flowers in the vase arranged?

   _____

3. Does the arrangement of the flowers affect your feeling about the painting? How?

   _____

   _____

> *Van Gogh chose a specific way to arrange the sunflowers. Similarly, authors must choose a way to arrange the information in their writing.*

Sharpen Your Reading Skills

RECOGNIZING PATTERNS OF ORGANIZATION

Language, both written and oral, is a reflection of the thought patterns of its native speakers. To read efficiently in a different language, it is important to understand the way writers organize their thoughts. You have already learned that in English, writers use supporting details to explain their main ideas. Supporting details (such as examples, facts, descriptions, reasons, explanations) are often organized in certain patterns. English writers use these patterns to arrange information in a clear and organized manner and to show relationships between ideas.

In this chapter, you will study four of the most common patterns of organization that writers in English use to present information.

1. Listing
2. Sequence (also called time order)
3. Cause and effect
4. Compare and contrast

Although much of what you read will be a combination of several patterns, learning to recognize the basic ones will help you understand and remember what you read.

Listing

One of the most common patterns of organizing information is to **list** details that explain or illustrate the main idea. In this pattern, the supporting details are listed as a series of reasons, examples, or facts.

Look for signal words that indicate an enumeration or listing pattern.

Signal Words for Lists

first	a variety	the main	for example	next	last
another	second	furthermore	numerous	many	also
a few	in addition	third	finally	several	

A. Read each paragraph. As you read, underline the signal words, and then answer the question that follows.

1.   There are three ways to start your subscription to *Health News Today*. The first way, and the fastest, is to call us toll-free at 1-800-555-5555 and place an order with a credit card. Another way is to place your order online. Finally, if you have access to a fax machine, you can fax a purchase order to us at 555-555-5555. As our thanks for placing your introductory order, you will receive our discounted price of 8 issues for $10 or 16 issues for $18. We look forward to hearing from you.

How many ways are there to start a subscription to *Health News Today*? _____

2.   There are several things you can do to protect your house or apartment from burglary, especially if you go away. It seems obvious, but the first thing you should do is make sure you have good locks on all your doors. Check to see that all your windows close tightly and lock. Another helpful and inexpensive thing you can do is make sure there is plenty of light at night, both inside and outside your house. Experts say that burglars do not like to work in light. Finally, make your home seem occupied. For example, turn the ringer on your phone off, ask a neighbor to collect your newspapers and mail, and put your TV and lights on timers. Remember, the more difficult you make access to your home the better. Most burglars will move on if it takes more than 4 minutes to get in.

How many ways to protect your home from burglary does the author mention? _____

Sequence

 Another pattern authors use is **sequence**. Authors use this pattern when they want to organize events chronologically (according to the order in which they occurred over time) or when they explain the steps of a process.

To show time relationships, authors often use signal words to guide the reader from one event or step to the next.

Also look for dates, seasons, days of the week, and times.

B. Read the following paragraphs. As you read, underline the signal words and think about the order of events. Then number the details that follow each paragraph in the correct sequence.

1. Mothers have been honored on Mother's Day since the 1600s, but fathers have had a special day only since 1910. The idea for a day to honor fathers originated with a woman in Spokane, Washington, named Sonora Dodd. Mrs. Dodd wanted to honor and thank her father for all he had done for her and her five brothers and sisters. The city council in Spokane liked the idea of a day to celebrate fathers. Spokane celebrated its first Father's Day on June 19, 1910. The idea quickly spread all over the country. By 1924, President Calvin Coolidge chose the third Sunday in June as a national day to honor fathers. In 1972, President Richard Nixon made it official.

    _____ Spokane celebrated its first Father's Day.

    _____ President Richard Nixon made Father's Day official.

    _____ Mrs. Dodd wanted to honor and thank her father.

    _____ President Calvin Coolidge chose the third Sunday in June as a day to honor fathers.

2. The life cycle of a frog has several stages. A frog begins its life in water as a tiny egg surrounded by a ball of jelly. Ten days later, a baby frog, called a tadpole, hatches from the egg and swims out of the jelly ball. The tadpole breathes with gills (like a fish) that are on the outside of its body. It has a long tail that it uses to swim. The tadpole grows for about five weeks, and then it begins to change. The tadpole grows back legs and its outside gills begin to disappear. One week after the back legs form, the tadpole develops lungs that can breathe air on land. Then in ten to twelve weeks, the tadpole grows front legs and starts to lose its tail. Once it finishes growing and has lost its tail, it is considered an adult frog.

    _____ The tadpole grows back legs and begins to lose its gills.

    _____ It develops lungs.

    _____ A tadpole, with gills and a tail, hatches from a tiny egg.

    _____ It loses its tail.

    _____ It grows front legs.

Cause and Effect

 When writers want to analyze the reasons (**causes** or factors) and/or the results (**effects**, disadvantages, benefits) of something they use a cause-and-effect pattern.

Look for signal words that indicate a cause-and-effect pattern.

Signal Words for Cause and Effect

because	due to	therefore	results in	causes
effects	because of	for this reason	leads to	as a result
consequently	result	thus	brings about	since

C. Underline the signal words in the paragraph. Then make a list of the effects.

The most famous snowstorm in American history, the Blizzard of 1888, has acquired an almost legendary status. Although there have been many heavier snowfalls as well as significantly lower temperatures, this blizzard's combination of inclement conditions—40 to 50 inches of snow in 36 hours with 48-mph winds—has been unmatched in 110 years. And the effects were disastrous. The "Great White Hurricane," as it was called, paralyzed the East Coast from the Chesapeake Bay to Maine. As a result of the blizzard, telegraph and telephone wires snapped, isolating New York, Boston, Philadelphia, and Washington for days. Two hundred ships were grounded, and at least 100 seamen died. Fire stations were powerless, and property loss from fire alone was estimated at $25 million. Overall, more than 400 deaths were directly or indirectly caused by the blizzard.

Effects:

_____   _____

_____   _____

_____   _____

D. Some paragraphs explain both the causes and the effects of something. Read the following paragraph and then complete the chart that follows it.

Many historians have studied the various factors that contributed to the gradual fall of the Roman Empire. Most would agree that the decline in population was one of the most important. At its height (from 27 B.C. to 180 A.D.) the population of Rome was about 70 million. By the end of the fourth century this number had fallen to about 50 million. What led to the decline in population? Famine, diseases, and a declining birthrate were some of the factors. In addition, many soldiers died in the constant wars fought by the Roman army. In what ways was the empire affected by the fall in population? Population loss meant fewer farmers to feed the people of Rome. It also meant fewer soldiers to fight in the army. Finally, there were fewer people to pay taxes to keep the government going.

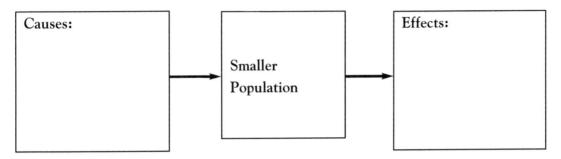

Compare and Contrast

 Another pattern writers use is **compare and contrast**. Writers use this pattern to show how two things (people, places, and so on) are similar or different.

Look for signals to indicate that similarities are being compared.

Signal Words for Comparisons			
like	likewise	similarly	both
by the same token	also	equally	similarities
just like	equally		

Look for signals to show that differences are being contrasted.

Signal Words for Contrasts			
on the other hand	in contrast	however	different
in spite of	conversely	despite	on the contrary
instead of	rather than	though	different from
unlike	even though	whereas	although

Also look for comparative forms of adjectives and adverbs (*cheaper*, *more difficult*, and so on).

E. Read the paragraph. Underline the signal words and complete the chart.

Psychologists have observed that people learn in different ways, absorbing information through different senses. Most people can be classified as either visual learners or auditory learners. Visual learners learn most efficiently with their eyes. They take in information by observing visual cues or by reading information. Auditory learners, on the other hand, learn with their ears. They understand information best by listening to oral clues and hearing information. These two types of learners would use different processes in learning a foreign language, for example. Visual learners learn a new language most effectively by reading books, newspapers, or magazines. They benefit from looking at diagrams, charts, and pictures and reading written directions. In contrast, auditory learners benefit from listening to lectures and CDs, watching movies or television, or having a conversation in the second language. They respond best to precise oral directions and explanations. Of course, most learners use both visual and auditory methods. Researchers report, though, that most of us are likely to use one sense more effectively than the other.

	Visual Learners	Auditory Learners
What they use to learn	eyes	ears
How they take in information		
How they learn a new language		

Using Headings

Headings often give clues about the pattern of organization a writer is using. Knowing the pattern can help you anticipate what the author is writing about in each section of the reading.

Read the headings and circle the letter of the pattern of organization the author will probably use.

1. Two Views on Government: Thomas Hobbes versus John Locke
   a. sequence
   b. listing
   c. compare and contrast
   d. cause and effect

2. Women's Contributions to the Enlightenment
   a. sequence
   b. listing
   c. compare and contrast
   d. cause and effect

3. The Stages of Culture Shock
   a. sequence
   b. listing
   c. compare and contrast
   d. cause and effect

4. A Look at the Effects of Industrialization
   a. sequence
   b. listing
   c. compare and contrast
   d. cause and effect

5. How to Treat a Burn
   a. sequence
   b. listing
   c. compare and contrast
   d. cause and effect

6. Why Did the League of Nations Fail?
   a. sequence
   b. listing
   c. compare and contrast
   d. cause and effect

7. The Life Cycle of a Butterfly
   a. sequence
   b. listing
   c. compare and contrast
   d. cause and effect

8. Part-Time and Full-Time Program Similarities
   a. sequence
   b. listing
   c. compare and contrast
   d. cause and effect

PRACTICE WITH PATTERNS OF ORGANIZATION

Read each paragraph, underline the signal words, and circle the letter of the pattern of organization the author used.

1.   Scientists acquire knowledge through a process called the scientific method. The steps of the scientific method provide scientists with an orderly way of gaining information. The first step in the scientific method is called observation. At this point, the scientist observes some aspect of the universe and uses the observations to ask a question or state a problem to investigate. After that, the scientist does research to learn as much as possible about the problem. Next, the scientist forms a hypothesis (an explanation that would explain the observations) and uses the hypothesis to make predictions. Then the scientist tests the hypothesis by doing experiments. Facts are collected, recorded, and analyzed. Finally, the scientist makes a conclusion based on the facts from the experiments.

   a. sequence
   b. listing
   c. compare and contrast
   d. cause and effect

2.	There are many benefits of reading books aloud to young children. First, reading aloud is a wonderful opportunity for parents to spend time in close contact with their children. After a busy day, reading a book can be a relaxing way for a family to slow down and communicate. Another important feature of reading aloud is that many books have thoughtful ideas or moral messages. Parents and children can explore these concepts together. In addition, listening to stories helps a child learn vocabulary and sentence structure. Moreover, some researchers believe that reading aloud to a child actually stimulates learning and benefits brain development. Studies have shown that children do better in school when their parents have read to them frequently. Psychologists, doctors, teachers, and librarians encourage parents to read aloud on a regular basis to assist the development of the child and build close family relationships.

a. sequence
b. listing
c. compare and contrast
d. cause and effect

3.	The availability of videotapes and VCRs revolutionized movie viewing. No longer was it necessary to watch a movie in a theater. Instead, it became possible to watch a movie at home. However, videotapes have been nearly replaced by digital videodiscs, or DVDs. DVDs are different from videotapes in several ways. First, the discs are much smaller than videotapes and take up less space to store. Another important difference is that DVDs are clearer, with better quality picture and sound. In addition, unlike a videotape it is not necessary to rewind DVDs. DVDs also have the option of scene selection so that a viewer can easily find a certain part of the movie to watch. Finally, many DVDs have special features, such as extra scenes not shown in the original movie and interviews with the director and actors, which videotapes do not have.

a. sequence
b. listing
c. compare and contrast
d. cause and effect

4.	If you are in the market for a new car, you should think about the possibility of buying a hybrid car instead of a traditional gasoline-powered car. Take a minute to consider the differences. Hybrid cars use a combination of two or more sources of power, usually gasoline and electric power. In comparison with gasoline-powered cars, hybrids have smaller engines with fewer parts. Another difference is that hybrids are usually lighter in weight. The smaller engine and lighter body materials result in a car that weighs less than a gasoline-powered car of similar size. Hybrid cars also use energy more efficiently. When a driver steps on the brakes to slow down, the braking energy can be used to recharge the battery. Hybrid cars get much better gas mileage than traditional cars, saving money on gasoline bills. For many drivers of hybrid cars, the most important difference is the greater benefit to the environment. Hybrid cars not only use less gas, but they produce fewer harmful emissions, cutting down on air pollution. These cars release significantly less carbon dioxide, carbon monoxide, nitrogen oxides, and hydrocarbons into the air.

a. sequence
b. listing
c. compare and contrast
d. cause and effect

5. One of the most important developments of the Renaissance was the invention of the printing press in the 1450s. This invention had three main effects. First, it made bookmaking much cheaper. Therefore, more people could afford to buy books, and as a result, literacy increased. Second, the process of bookmaking became faster, so many more books could be published on a variety of subjects. Third, the printing press made it possible for scholars to have access to books by other authors and to exchange information more easily.

a. sequence
b. listing
c. compare and contrast
d. cause and effect

6. We often think of the heart as the most vital human organ. The heart is a muscular organ that pumps blood throughout the body, delivering oxygen and transforming carbon dioxide. Blood with oxygen is pumped away from the heart through blood vessels called arteries. After traveling through the body, the blood then circulates back to the heart carrying carbon dioxide in other blood vessels called veins. Inside the heart, the carbon dioxide is taken out of the blood and oxygen is returned. The process of blood flowing in and out of the heart is continual.

a. sequence
b. listing
c. compare and contrast
d. cause and effect

7. A recent report from the National Academy of Sciences says that most of the oil pollution in the water along the North American coast is not caused by oil tankers and oil rigs at sea. Most of the oil pollution comes from sources on land. For example, when it rains, oil that lawnmowers leave on lawns and that cars leave on streets and parking lots runs off. This runoff is carried by streams and storm drains to rivers, bays, and the sea, killing marine life along the way. According to the report, 85 percent of the 29 million gallons of marine oil pollution in North American comes from individual users—not the oil industry.

a. sequence
b. listing
c. compare and contrast
d. cause and effect

8.	Elvis Presley was born in 1935 in Tupelo, Mississippi, and moved with his family to Memphis, Tennessee, in 1948. During his early childhood, Elvis heard a lot of country music, rhythm and blues, and gospel singing. In his teens, Presley taught himself to play the guitar. Although he never had any musical training, Elvis liked to play the songs he heard on the radio. By 1956, Elvis had a business manager and a major success when the song "Heartbreak Hotel" reached number 1 on the pop charts. He began getting recording offers, concert dates, television appearances, and movie contracts, and he soon became a national celebrity. Elvis was called a rock 'n' roll artist, but he was greatly influenced by the musical styles he heard in his childhood. Although teenagers loved his performing style, their parents did not. As time went on, however, Elvis became popular with older people, too. Eventually he stopped giving concerts and spent his time on his family and home at Graceland. He began recording slower songs and making movies. Elvis Presley remained popular and influential through the 1960s and 1970s until his sudden death in 1977. Even now there continues to be great interest in "the King of Rock 'n' Roll."

   a. sequence
   b. listing
   c. compare and contrast
   d. cause and effect

9.	The coldest places on earth, the Arctic (northern) and Antarctic (southern) polar regions, lie at opposite ends of the planet. Although both regions experience some of the harshest weather anywhere, the Antarctic is colder and windier than the Arctic. Temperatures in Antarctica have been recorded as low as −120°F (−84°C). Most of Antarctica is covered all year with a thick layer of ice. However, during the summer months, the Arctic is mostly free of snow and ice cover. This makes the Arctic climate more hospitable to humans than the climate of the ice-locked Antarctic continent. In fact, the Arctic region has been inhabited by humans for almost 20,000 years, whereas Antarctica has no permanent group of people. The only people who live there are scientists who work at research stations for part of the year. The milder climate in the Arctic is also better for plant growth and animal life. Several species of larger mammals, including polar bears, wolves, and foxes, as well as a variety of plants live in the Arctic area. In addition, thousands of migratory birds and other animals go to the Arctic to feed and raise their young in the summer. The Antarctic, however, has almost no plant and animal life year-round. It is so cold that only two species of flowering plants survive there. Still, several types of animals, such as penguins and seals and whales, live in Antarctica at certain times of the year.

   a. sequence
   b. listing
   c. compare and contrast
   d. cause and effect

> **TIP** Understanding the way the material will be presented—its pattern of organization—will help you put the main ideas and details into perspective. It will also prepare you to understand what you read.

Be an Active Reader

READING 1: **Race to the End of the Earth**

BEFORE YOU READ

Activate Your Background Knowledge

A. Discuss these questions with a partner.

1. Reread paragraph 9 in Practice with Patterns of Organization on page 102. What do you already know about Antarctica (where the South Pole is located)? Where is Antarctica located? Why do you think it would be difficult to get there? Do you think it would be difficult to travel around in Antarctica?

2. What qualities do you think makes someone a good leader of a difficult journey?

3. Why do you think someone would want to be an explorer?

Preview and Predict

B. Read the title and headings of the article on pages 105–107. Then look at the map and the pictures. Read the captions. Do you know anything about either of the two men? Have you ever ridden a sled or been on skis? Have you ever traveled through a difficult environment? Make some predictions about what topics might be discussed in the article and write them on the lines.

_____

_____

_____

_____

_____

_____

Preview the Vocabulary

C. The words and phrases in the box are boldfaced in the article. Complete the Vocabulary Chart with words from the box. If necessary, use your dictionary.

> **Words to Watch**
>
> | | | |
> |---|---|---|
> | used up | expedition | master |
> | brutal | toiled | weary |
> | blizzards | triumph | |

Vocabulary Chart	
Word	**Definition**
	an important victory or success, especially after a difficult struggle
	to become a ruler over another or to have control over something
	worked very hard on something for a long period of time
	long, heavy snowstorms with a lot of wind and snow
	a long and carefully organized trip, especially to a dangerous place or one that has not been visited before
	very cruel and violent
	very tired, especially after doing something for a long time
	used completely

Set a Purpose

You are going to read an article about two explorations to the South Pole. What do you want to find out about this topic? Write two questions you would like the article to answer.

1. _____

2. _____

As you read the article, underline the words and phrases that signal contrasts. Think about how the two expeditions were different.

Race to the End of the Earth

1   Blinded by **blizzards**, two groups of explorers struggled over a harsh, frozen landscape in 1911. The Norwegian explorer Roald Amundsen led one group. Captain Robert Falcon Scott, a British naval officer, led the other group. Each wanted to be the first to reach the South Pole. Who would win?

Reaching the South Pole Was Very Difficult

2   Explorers had reached the North Pole in 1909. But reaching the South Pole was much more difficult. It lies deep within Antarctica. All but a tiny portion of Antarctica is covered by ice. Temperatures can drop to –120°F (–84°C) in winter, and strong winds blow across the plateau, a large, flat open area. Winter darkness lasts 6 months. Whoever could **master** this harsh environment would receive worldwide fame and admiration.

Roald Amundsen relied on dog sleds and skis on his expedition in the Antarctic.

Different Preparations

3   Although both **expedition** leaders had long been preparing for the race to the South Pole, each did it in a different way. Norwegian Roald Amundsen had spent much time in the far north, and he planned to rely on sled dogs and skis. But Scott didn't want to rely on sled dogs and special equipment. Although he brought some dogs to Antarctica, he mainly wanted to use 19 ponies and three gasoline-powered sledges, or sturdy sleds. His plan was for his team to "man-haul," or carry, their supplies along the final portion of the route. The two leaders even had different ideas about diet. Scott's men would rely on canned meat, but Amundsen's men would eat plenty of fresh seal meat. (Fresh meat is a better source of vitamin C, which prevents scurvy, a painful and sometimes deadly disease.)

Captain Robert Falcon Scott used ponies and gasoline-powered sleds.

(continued)

4   After making long sea voyages from Europe, Scott and Amundsen set up base camps on opposite edges of the Ross Ice Shelf. Each had mapped out a different route for reaching the South Pole from his base camp. Amundsen's route of 1,700 miles was shorter than Scott's route of 1,766 miles. Amundsen left base camp on October 20, 1911, with a party of four men. Scott, accompanied by a group of nine men, set off from his camp 11 days later. Four of his teammates had already gone ahead on the motorized sledges.

Scott Has Problems

5   Things went wrong for Scott from the beginning. The motorized sledges broke down and the men had to abandon them. Scott's men had to fight severe weather conditions. Blizzards struck and lasted several weeks into December. Scott's ponies were a poor choice for Antarctic travel as well. Their hooves sank deep into the snow, and their perspiration froze on their bodies, forming sheets of ice. (Dogs do not perspire; they pant.) On December 9, Scott's men shot the last of the surviving weak and frozen ponies. Two days later Scott sent his remaining dogs back to base camp along with several members of the expedition. Over the next month, most of the men returned to the camp. Scott's plan from here on was for the five men remaining to carry all the supplies the rest of the way to the Pole and back.

6   For Scott and his men, the journey was long and **brutal**. To cover only 10 miles (16 kilometers) each day, the team **toiled** like dogs—the dogs they no longer had. Food and fuel were in

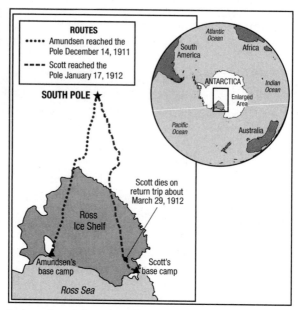

Each explorer followed a different route to reach the South Pole.

short supply, so the men lacked the energy they needed for such a difficult task.

Amundsen Has an Easier Trip

7   By comparison, Amundsen had a much easier journey. Amundsen's team crossed some mountains, then began to travel over a plateau they later named the Devil's Ballroom. On skis, with well-fed dogs pulling their supply sleds, Amundsen and his men swept across the plateau. The going was smooth for them, and the weather was fine. At three o'clock on December 14, Amundsen stopped to look at his navigation instruments. He was at the South Pole!

8   When Roald Amundsen raised the Norwegian flag at the South Pole, Scott and his men were still some 360 miles (580 kilometers) away. More than a month later,

Amundsen found that dog sleds were good for travel in the Antarctic.

food, and some fuel they had brought to build fires had leaked from its containers. Unfortunately, the markers showing the places where Scott had left extra supplies were covered with blowing snow. The men had scurvy and frostbite, and while they were trying to find the markers along their route back to base camp, they **used up** valuable time. All through January and February the team struggled on. On February 17, a team member collapsed and died. One month later another man walked into a blizzard and disappeared. Within two weeks the others, including Scott, had died—only 11 miles (18 kilometers) from a supply of food and fuel.

on January 17, 1912, the last members of the **weary**, disappointed British team finally reached the Pole. They saw the Norwegian flag and a note from Amundsen asking them to pass along news of his **triumph** if he failed to make it home.

Scott's Return Trip

9   Worse was yet to come on Scott's return trip. He and his men did not have enough

Amundsen's Return Trip

10   The Norwegian team had an easy trip back. They actually gained weight while sledding and skiing. Amundsen was already in the United States on a lecture tour when a reporter told him of Scott's fate. "Horrible, horrible," he exclaimed. He would gladly have given up the honor of victory, he said, if he could have "saved Scott his terrible death." But the unforgiving Antarctic had had the final word.

AFTER YOU READ

Check Your Comprehension

A. True or false? Write T (True) or F (False) next to each of the following statements. If a statement is false, rewrite it to make it true.

_____ **1.** Ponies and dogs are both good choices for Antarctic travel.

_____ **2.** Amundsen's party had a relatively smooth trip to the South Pole but a difficult trip back.

_____ **3.** The two men planned to follow the same route to reach their destination.

(continued)

_____ 4. Many of Scott's decisions turned out to be good ones.

_____ 5. The South Pole is more difficult to reach than the North Pole.

_____ 6. The disease called scurvy is caused by a vitamin C deficiency.

_____ 7. Both expedition parties were made up of four men.

_____ 8. Canned meat is not as nutritious as fresh meat.

Complete the Chart

B. Think about the differences between the two expeditions and complete the chart below.

	Amundsen's Expedition	Scott's Expedition
Diet	plenty of fresh seal meat	
Animals and equipment		
Number of men on the team		
Weather conditions		
Method of transportation		
Return trip		

Use Context Clues

C. Use context clues to guess the meaning of the words that follow. Look back at the context of each word. The paragraph number is given in paratheses. Write a definition or synonym of each word or phrase. Then compare answers with a partner.

1. plateau (para. 2)

   _____

2. sledges (para. 3)

   _____

3. man-haul (para. 3)

   _____

4. scurvy (para. 3)

   _____

5. party (para. 4)

   _____

Test Your Vocabulary

D. Complete each of the sentences that follow with the best word from the box.
Be sure to use the correct form of the word.

used up	expedition	master	brutal
blizzards	triumph	weary	toiled

1. Lilly _____ all semester on her thesis.

2. We got stuck in the _____ and had to abandon our car in the snow.

3. I feel _____ from working on this project for so long.

4. Winning the gold medal was a personal _____ for Julia after all the problems she's had with her knee.

5. The winters are _____ in that part of the world.

6. He led a(n) _____ to the top of Mt. Kilimanjaro.

7. Who _____ all my toothpaste?

8. Coli was determined to _____ the advanced slope, so he skied down it many times.

Pronoun Reference

E. Read the following sentences from the reading. Notice each underlined pronoun and write the noun(s) that it refers to.

1. But reaching the South Pole was much more difficult. <u>It</u> lies deep within Antarctica. It = _____

2. The motorized sledges broke down and the men had to abandon <u>them</u>. them = _____

3. By comparison, Amundsen had a much easier journey. <u>His</u> route was also shorter. His = _____

4. Scott's ponies were a poor choice for Antarctic travel as well. <u>Their</u> hooves sank deep into the snow. Their = _____

5. Amundsen was already in the United States on a lecture tour when a reporter told <u>him</u> of Scott's fate. him = _____

6. Fresh meat is a better source of vitamin C, <u>which</u> prevents scurvy, a painful and sometimes deadly disease. which = _____

Sum It Up

Write a one-paragraph summary of "Race to the End of the Earth." Remember to include only main ideas from the article in your summary.

_____

_____

_____

_____

Share Your Thoughts

A. Work with a small group. Discuss these questions.

1. What do you think motivates people to seek glory through adventure and exploration?

2. What obstacles did the Antarctic explorers face during their journey? How did they overcome them?

3. Are you interested in going to the South Pole? Why or why not?

4. If you were to follow Scott's or Amundsen's route to the South Pole, who would you want to accompany your team through Antarctica (a doctor, for example)? What would you take with you? What kind of research would you like to do there?

5. Do you agree or disagree with those who feel that neither scientists nor tourists should go to remote places such as Antarctica because humans disturb the ecology of the area? Why or why not?

B. Choose one of the questions in Exercise A and write a paragraph about it.

_____

_____

_____

_____

_____

_____

READING 2: Lance Armstrong

You have just read an article about two men who faced many challenges to reach their goal. Now you are going to read an article about another man, Lance Armstrong, who also faced many challenges to achieve his goal.

BEFORE YOU READ

Activate Your Background Knowledge

A. Discuss these questions with a partner.

1. Have you ever been in a race? What kind? How did you prepare for the race?

2. Have you ever watched the bicycle race Tour de France in person or on TV?

3. Do you like to ride bikes? Do you prefer riding a bike, driving a car, or walking somewhere? Why?

Preview and Predict

B. Preview the article on pages 112–114 by reading the title, subtitle, and headings. Look at the photograph and read the caption. Then make some predictions about the article. Write your predictions on the lines.

_____

_____

_____

_____

Preview the Vocabulary

C. The words and phrases in the box are boldfaced in the article. Use context clues to guess the meaning of the boldfaced words and phrases in the exercise. Write definitions or synonyms of the words and phrases. If necessary, use your dictionary. Then compare answers with a partner.

Words to Watch		
narrow margin	perilous	oppressive
run out	pileup	paid off
turn to	pinnacle	potential

1. The icy highway was closed for hours after the accident. The police reported a ten-car **pileup** on the highway.

   _____

2. Louis **turned to** politics after he finished law school.

   _____

3. Yoshio reached the **pinnacle** of success as a writer at the age of 45 when he won the Pulitzer Prize for Poetry.

   _____

4. She was told that she had great **potential** as a pianist. To achieve her full potential, she needs to train with a master and practice hard every day.

   _____

5. A group of explorers made the **perilous** journey to the South Pole.

   _____

6. After years of winning, his luck finally began to **run out** when he lost two races in a row.

   _____

7. The final score was 107 to 106. We won by a **narrow margin**.

   _____

8. I was happy to hear about your promotion to vice president of the company. All your hard work has **paid off**.

   _____

9. We couldn't sleep because of the **oppressive** heat.

   _____

AS YOU READ

Think about the order of events in the article. Underline the signal words that show sequence.

Lance Armstrong
Overcoming Obstacles and Breaking Records

Early Challenges, Early Success

1   Born in Texas in 1971, Lance Armstrong was raised by his mother and had no contact with his father. He entered cycling competitions at a young age and had already started training with the U.S. National Team in his last year of high school. In 1991 Lance became the U.S. National Amateur Champion. However, the

Few athletes have achieved as many victories as cyclist Lance Armstrong. Few have needed to overcome so many obstacles to achieve their victories.

following year, at his first professional race, Spain's Clasica San Sebastian, Lance finished in last place. Not discouraged, he went on to win the 1993 U.S. Pro Championship. Lance has said that it was his mother's example of hard work and persistence that motivated him not to give up even when he lost an important race. In his autobiography, *It's Not About the Bike*, Lance said that his mother always told him to turn every obstacle into an opportunity. Eventually, in 1995, Lance Armstrong became the first American to win at San Sebastian.

An Unexpected Crisis

2   Lance's hard work and talent had enabled him to rise to the top of the cycling world, and in 1996 he was ranked number one. His remarkable success almost came to an end when a crisis occurred later that year. Lance was diagnosed with cancer and doctors predicted that he had little chance of recovery.

However, Lance was determined to fight the cancer. After a series of medical treatments, he recovered his health, and within a year he was able to begin training again. With a new perspective on life, Lance not only concentrated on cycling, but he also **turned to** helping others. He established the Lance Armstrong Foundation to promote cancer research and to help people diagnosed with cancer to manage their health. To fund the foundation, Lance created the Ride for the Roses, an annual cycling event in Austin, Texas.

The Cycling World's Greatest Challenge

3   By 1999, Armstrong had won several important races and had joined the U.S. Postal Service cycling team. They entered the cycling world's most important competition, the Tour de France, a **perilous** three-week race through France, including the Alps and the Pyrenees mountains. Early in the race, Lance won the right to wear the *maillot jaune*, the yellow jersey that distinguishes the overall leading rider of the previous lap. Lance and his teammates won the Tour de France, becoming the first American team to do so. Lance's victory was an inspiration to everyone who has faced a challenge in life and was especially inspiring to cancer survivors. The staff and patients at the Texas Medical Center, where Lance had been treated, watched his race on TV and cheered his victory.

Misfortune Strikes Again

4   Lance continued to push himself as an athlete to reach his full **potential**. He followed a rigorous training schedule. Unfortunately, his luck **ran out** in 2000,

(continued)

when he was hit by a car while training in France. He suffered from a broken bone in his back, but he recovered and soon went on to race again. With the U.S. Postal Service Team, Lance continued to dominate the Tour de France, winning in 2000, 2001, and 2002. The team had to overcome bad weather conditions and numerous crashes to win these races. Then, in 2003, at the 100-year anniversary of the Tour de France, Lance faced the opportunity to win a fifth Tour de France victory. If he succeeded, he would become only the fifth cyclist in history to earn five Tour de France titles. In addition, he would match the record of Spain's Miguel Indurain, the only man to win five Tour de France races in successive years, 1991–1995.

The Most Difficult Race

5   The 2003 race proved to be very difficult. Riding in **oppressive** heat, Lance encountered one difficulty after another. For most of the race he suffered from stomach flu and he crashed twice during the race. Furthermore, there were many **pileups** of fallen riders that Lance narrowly avoided. Nonetheless, the U.S. Postal Service Team won by a **narrow margin** of 61 seconds. Lance Armstrong had won a fifth Tour de France victory in his most hard-fought race ever. Cycling fans throughout the world celebrated this accomplishment and said he had reached the **pinnacle** of his career.

Breaking the Record

6   Immediately after Lance Armstrong had won a fifth Tour de France race, excitement began to build about the possibility of a sixth victory. No man in history had ever reached this goal. With his fifth successive Tour de France championship, Lance matched the record of Miguel Indurain. Now he set out with a new goal, to win still another Tour de France race. During the next year, Lance focused on training primarily for this event and chose not to participate in other races. His focus and hard training **paid off**, and in 2004 Lance Armstrong won a record-breaking sixth Tour de France victory with the U.S. Postal Service Team.

Appreciation of Life

7   Lance Armstrong has won many races and many honors, including the *Sports Illustrated* "Sportsman of the Year" and the Associated Press "Male Athlete of the Year" awards. However, Lance is modest about his success. He gives credit to his teammates often, acknowledging earlier mistakes in his attitude toward racing. He expresses gratitude for the lessons he has learned as a cancer survivor, which helped him to appreciate life. Through his impressive cycling victories, his astonishing recovery from illness, and his work with the foundation, Lance Armstrong stands out as an example of determination, courage, and compassion.

AFTER YOU READ

Complete the Timeline

A. Work with a partner. Make a list of the important events in Lance Armstrong's life. Use the list to complete the timeline.

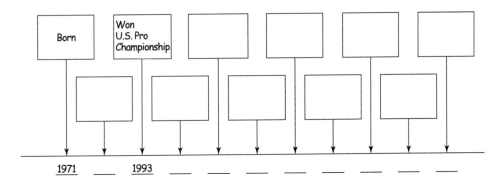

Sharpen Your Vocabulary Skills

WORD PARTS

Remember that suffixes often indicate the function (noun, verb, adjective, or adverb) of a word in a sentence. Study the chart of common suffixes that are used to make verbs.

Verb Suffixes		
Suffix	Meaning	Examples
-ate	*to make, have, become*	differentiate, motivate
-ize	*to make, have, become*	memorize, modernize
-en	*to make, have, become*	frighten, toughen
-ify	*to make, have, become*	certify, magnify

Add the correct suffix to the root word in each of the following sentences. Be sure to use the correct form of the word.

1. Your essay is too complicated. You need to (simple) _____.

2. This switch (active) _____ the machine.

3. I need to (sharp) _____ this pencil before the test.

4. He was accused of (false) _____ the company records.

5. You need to sign this paper to (legal) _____ it.

6. We don't want to (alien) _____ children who already have problems at school.

Share Your Thoughts

Discuss these questions in small groups.

1. Many people think of Lance Armstrong as a true hero. How do you define a hero? Who do you consider a hero?

2. Lance Armstrong gained worldwide notice when he won the Tour de France. Why do you think this race is so well-known?

3. What difficulties has Lance Armstrong experienced during his life? How did he overcome the obstacles he faced?

Explore the Web

Work with a partner. Do some research on the Internet to learn about another famous person, such as Oprah Winfrey, Pat LaFontaine, Franklin D. Roosevelt, Helen Keller, or someone else you know of who has overcome obstacles. Begin the search by typing in the person's name and the word "biography" as key words. Explore two or three of the websites you found. Find a picture of the person and take notes about his or her life. Use your notes to make a timeline about the person's life.

Go Beyond the Text

Read the excerpt from the journal on page 117 that a woman wrote about her experience running in the Boston Marathon. Think of a goal that you have accomplished and write a journal entry that describes it.

April 19

Today was a great day! I met my goal of running five marathons before I turned 28. I ran the Boston Marathon today, and I did it in 4 hours and 7 minutes. This was the hardest and slowest marathon I've ever run because of the heat and the hills. Even the elite runners were slower this year because it was so hot.

I was in good physical shape because I started training in December and kept to my usual training regimen for

The Boston Marathon is the oldest annual marathon in the world.

the whole time. I ate healthy foods throughout my training period. I did my long runs on the weekends and short runs during the week. But all my training runs were in cold or mild temperatures. Even last week it was cold here! Yesterday the temperature was still in the fifties. But today dawned hot. It was 86 degrees this afternoon with 96 percent humidity and really hot out on the road. Of the 20,404 runners, more than 1,100 needed medical attention due to dehydration. Fortunately, there were plenty of medical tents and doctors to help them at every mile. I was careful to get water at every water station. The fire department opened fire hydrants, and I made sure to run close enough to get a shower to cool me off. The other thing that made this a hard race for me was that I did not expect so many hills! I knew about the famous Heartbreak Hill at about mile 20, but I never realized there were so many other hills at the beginning of the course.

Lots of people jump in and out of marathons to help their friends and cheer them on. My friend John ran with me from mile 17 to mile 22 for moral support, and when he dropped out, my boyfriend, Matt, jumped in to keep me going. He gave me the boost I needed because I was really beginning to drag. The fans all along the marathon route were great, too. If you put your name on your arms or shirt, they encouraged you by name. I'm so excited! I ran the Boston Marathon! Crossing that finish line was a thrill, but I think I'll retire from marathoning now. I'm tired, and sore, but proud. I did it!

CHAPTER 6

Make Inferences

Nighthawks by Edward Hopper

About the Artist

Edward Hopper (1882–1967) was born in Nyack, New York, and studied art in New York City. He was a famous American painter whose works marked a turning point in American realism, a style that tries to represent life as it really is. His paintings are often characterized by feelings of loneliness, mystery, and isolation. In this painting, *Nighthawks*, Hopper shows a cook behind the counter and three customers sitting in an all-night diner.

Look at Hopper's painting. Work with a partner and discuss what you see in the painting. Ask and answer these questions:

1. Are the people interacting with each other?

   _____

2. What time do you think it is? Early morning? Lunchtime? Late at night?

   _____

3. Do you see any way to get into or out of the diner?

   _____

4. What do you think Hopper is trying to tell us about the people? How do you think they feel? Why? _____

   _____

Although Hopper doesn't tell us directly what the people in the painting are feeling, we can make guesses based on the information in the picture. Like artists, writers don't always state directly everything they want you to know. Often, they only suggest ideas by giving hints and clues. They expect you to figure out some things on your own. In other words, they want you to make inferences.

Sharpen Your Reading Skills

MAKING INFERENCES

An **inference** is an educated guess based on information the author gives you. The ability to make inferences is a very important reading skill, but we also make inferences, or educated guesses, all the time in our everyday lives. That is, we believe something is true even though we don't have direct proof. For example, suppose your friend calls you and says, "I'm so <u>disappointed</u>. The game was so close until the last few seconds. Too bad we didn't make that last basket. I was sure the ball was going to go in." You can infer that your friend's team lost the basketball game even though she never stated so directly. To make good inferences when you are reading, you need to combine the clues in the reading with information you already know from your own life. This is similar to guessing the meaning of a word using context clues. You are making inferences then, too.

Read the following paragraph about a man's morning and make an inference about the man. Underline all the words that relate to doing things quickly.

Peter stared at the clock and then flew out of bed. He pulled a shirt and pair of pants from his closet and quickly got dressed. He stepped into his shoes but forgot to put on his socks. After making a quick effort to brush his teeth, he glanced in the mirror but didn't stop to wash his face or comb his hair. Grabbing his briefcase, Peter ran out of his apartment and raced to the elevator. After waiting for just 30 seconds, he gave up and instead ran down the stairs. He rushed out of the building, started running down the street, and finally jumped into a taxi.

The words you underlined are all indicators of someone in a hurry. Use these words as clues to help you choose the best inference you can make about Peter based on the information in the paragraph.

Example

a. Peter is a forgetful and careless person.

(b.) Peter is late and in a hurry to get somewhere.

c. Peter is a person who doesn't like to waste time.

A. Circle the letter of the inference you can make based on the information in the paragraph.

1. In the new mayor's speech, she explained how she would improve life in the city. She promised to hire more police to patrol the streets and more security guards to protect public buildings. In addition, she said that she would ask the state government to pass stricter gun legislation to control the number of guns in the city. Drug abuse was another topic the mayor addressed in her speech. The mayor was well received by the audience, who applauded her proposals.

   a. The mayor has very little experience in government.
   b. The mayor is worried about winning the next election.
   c. The mayor believes that crime is a serious problem in this city.

2. Robert looked up at the number on the building and then pulled out a piece of paper from his briefcase. He glanced down at the paper in his hand and then looked back up to check the number again. With his hands shaking a bit, he put the paper back in the briefcase. He muttered a few words to himself and hesitated for a minute or so. Then Robert started to walk away from the building. He paused, slowly turned, and then walked back to the door. Seeing his reflection in the glass window, he patted down his hair and adjusted his tie. Finally, Robert took a deep breath, stood up straight, and walked through the door.

   a. Robert is nervous about an appointment.
   b. Robert is entering a hospital.
   c. Robert is a very neat and careful person.

3. The South Beach diet, the Perricone prescription, and the Atkins diet are popular diets designed by prominent doctors. If followed over time, these diets reportedly can result in substantial weight loss. Supporters of these nutritional plans also claim that they have other health benefits and can prevent disease. Although there are differences in the three diets, all have low-carbohydrate menus,

restricting carbohydrates such as potatoes, rice, bread, and pasta. Many restaurants now offer low-carbohydrate selections for those who are dieting. Each of these diet plans has devoted followers who have successfully lost weight.

a. Eating a large amount of carbohydrates can cause weight gain.
b. Most Americans need to lose weight.
c. Most doctors believe that potatoes, rice, bread, and pasta are unhealthy foods that should never be eaten.

4. *American Idol*, a reality show on TV, became an instant sensation when it first appeared. The program features amateur singers, not professionals, who compete against each other in a singing contest. Their performances are evaluated by a panel of critics, who are sometimes quite negative. On each episode of the television program, viewers watching the show vote for their favorite singers by telephone, and then the singers with the least votes are cut. Finally, two contestants are left, and the viewers choose their favorite to become an "American idol." Many of the winners and finalists have gone on to become popular entertainers.

a. There aren't many professional singers, so Americans like to listen to amateurs.
b. Americans enjoy singing competitions.
c. *American Idol* is the best way for singers to start their careers.

5. No baseball team has been more successful than the New York Yankees. The team has won the World Series twenty-six times. Yankee baseball players such as Babe Ruth, Mickey Mantle, Yogi Berra, and Joe DiMaggio are legendary figures in baseball history. However, this fame and success has come at a price. There is some resentment against the Yankees, perhaps because of their numerous victories. Many sports fans like to support the "underdogs," or those less likely to win. Some fans have complained that the Yankees spend more money to buy the best players, making it difficult for other teams to compete. Although the Yankees have loyal and passionate fans, other baseball fans are always happy to see the Yankees lose.

a. Success can bring criticism and a lack of support.
b. In most games, the Yankees are the "underdogs."
c. The Yankees are no longer a successful team.

6. Isadora Duncan was one of the first dancers to break away from classical ballet and experiment with style and technique. Often called the "Mother of Modern Dance," she became one of the first great modern dancers and choreographers, or composers of dance. Born in San Francisco in 1878, Duncan performed mostly in Europe and established several schools there. She was noted for her free and natural movements, often dancing in bare feet and flowing costumes. When a reporter asked her what the meaning was of her unique dances, Duncan answered, "If I could explain the meaning to you in words, I wouldn't have danced for hours."

a. Duncan chose modern dance because she wasn't very good at classical ballet.
b. American audiences didn't like her style of dance, so Duncan moved to Europe.
c. Duncan felt that the meaning of her dance was in the dance itself and could not be explained in words.

7. Some of the most prestigious American colleges and universities were established in the colonial period, before the War of Independence began in 1776. The first American college, Harvard, was established in 1636 near Boston, Massachusetts. William and Mary was founded in 1693 in Virginia. In the next century, Yale was established in 1701, the University of Pennsylvania in 1740, Princeton in 1746, Columbia in 1754, Brown in 1764, Rutgers in 1766, and Dartmouth in 1769. Attendance at these colleges was restricted to white males; women and blacks were not able to apply for admission.

   a. Women, blacks, and white men did not have equal rights during the colonial period.
   b. Most colleges were closed during the War of Independence.
   c. Colleges founded after 1776 were not very prestigious.

 TIP To make good inferences, look for clues the author gives and relate them to what you know from other experiences in your own life.

Be an Active Reader

READING 1: Fortune-Telling

BEFORE YOU READ

Activate Your Background Knowledge

A. Discuss these questions with a partner.

1. Have you ever had your fortune told? What method did the fortune-teller use?

2. What did you learn from the fortune-teller? Was he or she right?

3. Do you think fortune-telling is simply a form of entertainment or do you think it is something more?

4. Is fortune-telling popular in your native culture? Which methods are the most popular?

Preview and Predict

B. Read the title and headings of the article on pages 124–126. Look at the pictures and read the captions. Can you guess what the article will be about? Think of three topics that might be discussed in the article.

1. _____

2. _____

3. _____

Preview the Vocabulary

C. The words in the box are boldfaced in the article on pages 124–126. Complete the Vocabulary Chart with words from the box. If necessary, use your dictionary.

Words to Watch			
palm	horoscope	reveal	forecast
aspect	analyze	compatible	
subconscious	psychologist	superstition	

Vocabulary Chart	
Word	**Definition**
	to show something that was previously hidden
	one of the parts or features of a situation, idea, or problem
	a description of your character and things that will happen to you, based on the position of the stars and planets when you were born
	able to live or work successfully with someone else
	a belief not based on scientific knowledge but connected with old ideas about magic; a belief that some objects or actions are lucky and some are unlucky
	a person who is trained in the scientific study of the mind, and how it works, and how mental problems can be treated
	the inside surface of your hand between the base of your fingers and your wrist
	related to the part of your mind in which there are thoughts and feelings that you do not realize that you have
	to examine or think about something carefully in order to understand it
	to say what is likely to happen in the future, based on information you have now

Set a Purpose

You are going to read an article about fortune-telling. What do you want to find out about this topic? Write two questions you would like the article to answer.

1. _____

2. _____

AS YOU READ

As you read the article, think about the underlined words and phrases. Use context clues to guess the meaning of each word, and write it on the line given. Remember to look at the words and sentences that surround the underlined words. Think about the strategy (definitions, examples, similarity signals, contrast, or general sense of sentence) that helped you figure out the meaning of the word.

Fortune-Telling

1   What will the future bring? Adventure, an unexpected marriage, or a long journey? Methods of predicting the future through fortune-telling have existed for centuries. Although many people <u>dismiss</u> these practices as **superstitions**, others accept them, and fortune-telling remains popular in many cultures. From analyzing the formation of clouds to opening fortune cookies at a Chinese restaurant, people do numerous things to make predictions about the future.

> dismiss: _____

It's All in the Hands

2   Reading **palms** has long been a favorite method of fortune-telling. The shape of fingers, the appearance of fingernails, and in particular the lines of the palm are important features for interpretation. Some say that there are three main lines in the hand, the life line, heart line, and head line, revealing intellectual and emotional aspects of the person. Look at your own palm. Do you see the three <u>dominant</u> lines? Gypsies, or the

Reading palms is a popular way to tell someone's future.

Roma, are famous for their skill at reading palms. They are also well known for their ability to interpret the images they see when they look into a <u>crystal ball</u>, a magic glass ball that shows the future.

> dominant: _____
>
> crystal ball: _____

Coffee or Tea?

3   A method of fortune-telling using coffee is practiced throughout the world, especially in the Middle East. After the coffee is drunk, the fortune-teller turns the cup several times and then looks at the <u>coffee grounds</u>, the tiny pieces of coffee beans left in the cup. She analyzes the shapes of the coffee grounds, which supposedly have various meanings. For example, a shape like a tree at the bottom of the cup could mean that positive changes are coming. Similarly, a form that looks like fruit might <u>signify</u> prosperity or good fortune. Other shapes have more obvious

Can the pattern of tea leaves in the bottom of your cup predict your future?

| coffee grounds: _____ |
| signify: _____ |

meanings to fortune-tellers. A heart could **forecast** love, and a ring suggests a marriage in the future. The patterns of tea leaves in the bottom of a teacup are used in a similar manner as a means of fortune-telling.

Symbolic Images

4   Tarot cards are also used to predict the future and to **analyze** a person's character. Dating back to the fifteenth century in Italy and perhaps originating from somewhere in Asia, the cards are marked with various symbols and characters. A few cards are selected, and they supposedly **reveal aspects** of a person's personality, major influences in his or her life, and maybe the direction of future actions. It takes knowledge and skill to analyze the <u>significance</u> of the cards. The I-Ching, an ancient Chinese book with symbols, is somewhat similar to Tarot cards. It also requires <u>expertise</u> to interpret the meaning of the symbols.

| significance: _____ |
| expertise: _____ |

The Planets and Stars

5   From the earliest times, many cultures have shown interest in <u>astrology</u>, the study of how the movement of stars and planets affects human events. Still popular today, astrology utilizes the **horoscope**, or twelve signs of the Zodiac, and a description of your character and things that will happen to you based on the position of the stars and planets at the time of your birth. Some people use the horoscope to determine whether they are likely to get along with others in a relationship or even in a marriage. According to followers of astrology, some signs of the Zodiac are especially **compatible** and are more likely to result in a <u>harmonious</u> relationship, while others are incompatible and are likely to end up in a relationship filled with conflict. Some people read their horoscope on a daily basis in newspapers or websites for advice about whether they will experience good or bad luck and for suggestions for action to take in the future. To paraphrase the words of William Shakespeare, the famous sixteenth-century English writer, however, it is not in the stars to hold our destiny, but in ourselves.

| astrology: _____ |
| harmonious: _____ |

What Do Dreams Reveal?

6   Just as stars are considered by some to influence human actions, dreams are <u>regarded as</u> indicators of the future. Colors, images, and events occurring in dreams supposedly have special significance; some believe they reflect **subconscious** fears, concerns, or desires. Others believe that dreams can predict future events. For example, in Chinese legends, a dream of a rainbow predicts eventual good fortune. A number of modern **psychologists** encourage patients to write down their dreams as a way of analyzing their concerns or issues. In psychology, dreams are not viewed as definite predictors of future events but rather as a means of self-discovery, a way of reflecting on the direction of one's life.

(continued)

regarded as: _____

A Means of Exploration

7   How many people actually believe in fortune-telling? Some insist that they have encountered fortune-tellers who appear to have special <u>psychic</u> powers that enable them to "see" the future. Others reject any form of fortune-telling as false and ridiculous. Some religions forbid fortune-telling in any form. Quite a few people, though, seem to enjoy various types of fortune-telling as forms of entertainment. At any rate, it is likely that fortune-telling will continue to appeal to those curious about the future. If not taken too seriously, fortune-telling can be viewed as an attempt to evaluate choices and possibly as a path to self-discovery.

psychic: _____

AFTER YOU READ

Check Your Comprehension

A. True or false? Write T (True) or F (False) next to each of the following statements. If a statement is false, rewrite it to make it true.

_____ **1.** In the past, people did not practice fortune-telling.

_____ **2.** Tea leaves and coffee grounds are used in a similar way to tell the future.

_____ **3.** Fortune-telling is practiced all over the world.

_____ **4.** Tarot cards and the I-Ching both require expertise in interpreting the symbols.

_____ **5.** Fortune-telling practices are frequently dismissed as superstitions.

_____ **6.** Coffee grounds are used in the Middle East to predict the future.

_____ **7.** The twelve signs of the Zodiac refer to the position of the stars.

_____ **8.** There are only a few ways to predict the future.

_____ **9.** It is a known fact that dreams indicate future events.

_____ **10.** Reading palms is a relatively recent way of predicting the future.

Use Context Clues

B. Work with a partner and compare the definitions you each wrote for the underlined words in the article. Talk about the clues and strategy you used to come up with your definition. Then look up the words in a dictionary. How close was your guess to the dictionary definition? Do you think your strategy was successful? Why or why not?

Make Inferences

C. Put a check next to the inferences that you can make after reading "Fortune-Telling."

_____ 1. A woman who believes in astrology might read her horoscope to see if her personality is compatible with her boyfriend's.

_____ 2. William Shakespeare probably did not believe in astrology.

_____ 3. Some people read their horoscope or go to fortune-tellers just for fun.

_____ 4. The author believes that the shapes of coffee grounds are true predictors of the future.

_____ 5. An inexperienced person cannot interpret the meaning of Tarot cards.

_____ 6. Some psychologists believe that dreams can be valuable in analyzing a person's subconscious issues.

_____ 7. If you dream about a rainbow, you will have good fortune.

_____ 8. More people reject than accept fortune-telling as a valid way to predict the future.

Test Your Vocabulary

D. Complete each of the sentences that follow with the best word from the box. Be sure to use the correct form of the word.

palm	horoscope	reveal	forecast
aspect	analyze	compatible	
subconscious	psychologist	superstition	

1. The _____ believes that his patient has a fear of failing.

2. I want a new roommate. My roommate and I are not _____.

3. She held the coin in the _____ of her hand.

4. The X-ray _____ a broken bone in my arm.

5. My _____ predicts that I am going to be lucky in love.

6. They looked at every _____ of the problem before making a decision.

7. We need to _____ the information before we make a decision.

8. Do you believe in the old _____ that the number 13 is unlucky?

9. The memory of the fire was buried deep in my _____.

10. Warm weather has been _____ for this weekend.

Pronoun Reference

E. Read each of the following sentences from the article. Notice each underlined pronoun and look for the noun it refers to. Write the noun on the line.

1. Gypsies, or the Roma, are famous for their skill at reading palms. <u>They</u> are also well-known for their ability to interpret the images they see when they look into a crystal ball. They = _____

2. After the coffee is drunk, the fortune-teller turns the cup several times and then looks at the coffee grounds, the tiny pieces of coffee beans left in the cup. <u>She</u> analyzes the shapes of the coffee grounds, which supposedly have various meanings. She = _____

3. A few cards are selected, and <u>they</u> supposedly reveal aspects of a person's personality, major influences in his or her life, and maybe the direction of future actions. they = _____

4. Some signs of the Zodiac are especially compatible and are more likely to result in a harmonious relationship, while <u>others</u> are incompatible and are likely to end up in a relationship filled with conflict. others = _____

5. A number of modern psychologists encourage patients to write down their dreams as a way of analyzing <u>their</u> concerns or issues. their = _____

Sum It Up

Write a one-paragraph summary of "Fortune-Telling." Remember to include only main ideas from the article in your summary.

_____

_____

_____

_____

Share Your Thoughts

A. Work with a small group. Discuss these questions.

1. Do you agree with William Shakespeare's observation, "It is not in the stars to hold our destiny, but in ourselves"? Why or why not?

2. Have you ever dreamed about something that actually happened later? Describe the dream to the people in your group.

3. Do you think dreams are means of self-discovery? Why or why not?

4. Do you know anyone who claims to have psychic powers? Describe the person.

B. Choose one of the questions in Exercise A and write a paragraph about it.

_____

_____

_____

_____

READING 2: The Fortune Sellers

BEFORE YOU READ

Activate Your Background Knowledge

A. You have just read an article about fortune-tellers, people who make predictions about the future. Now you are going to read an article about fortune *sellers*, or people who make lots of money by making predictions about the future. The author, William Sherden, wrote a book called *The Fortune Sellers: The Big Business of Buying and Selling Predictions*. Look at the painting that is used on cover of the book and discuss what you see with a partner. Why do you think the publisher chose this painting for the cover?

The cover of Sherden's book shows *The Cheat*, a painting by Georges de La Tour.

B. Read the statements in the chart that follows. Do you agree or disagree with the statements? Check your response in the first two columns. You will check the last columns after you read.

Before You Read		Evaluate the Statements	After You Read	
Agree	Disagree	Statement	Agree	Disagree
		It is reasonable to pay for information about the future.		
		The use of modern technology has helped us accurately predict the future.		
		The business of making predictions is a multibillion-dollar industry		

C. Work with a partner. Discuss the statements and compare responses.

Preview and Predict

D. Read the title and look at the headings in the article on pages 132–133. Read the first sentence of each paragraph. This will help you get an overview of the article. Can you predict what the article will be about? Think of three topics that might be discussed in the article. Write the topics on the lines.

1. _____

2. _____

3. _____

Preview the Vocabulary

E. The words in the box are boldfaced in the article. Use context clues to guess the meaning of the boldfaced words and phrases in the exercise. Circle the letter of the correct definition or synonym of each word or phrase. If necessary, use your dictionary. Then compare answers with a partner.

> **Words to Watch**
>
> piece of cake   hottest   make a killing   accuracy
> charlatans   brightest   showers   commodities market
> expand   contract   stock market

1. This new palm pilot is the **hottest** item at the computer show. Everyone wants to buy one.
   a. newest and most exciting
   b. most complicated and expensive

2. If you invest wisely, you can make a lot of money in the **stock market**.
   a. grocery store
   b. place where parts of the ownership of companies are bought and sold

3. Jane's boyfriend **showers** her with compliments.
   a. gives a lot of something
   b. gives a bath

4. As more and more people moved to Texas in the 1960s, the population **expanded**.
   a. became larger
   b. became smaller

5. Don't put your sweater in the dryer. When wool yarn dries, it **contracts**.
   a. becomes larger
   b. becomes smaller

6. The test was a **piece of cake**. Everyone got all the answers right.
   a. very hard
   b. very easy

7. Jackson is the **brightest** student in the class. He always gets the highest grades.
   a. most intelligent
   b. funniest

8. He questioned the **accuracy** of the research results. Most of the data seemed wrong.
   a. expense
   b. correctness

9. We all knew Simon was a **charlatan** who pretended to have a medical degree and tried to sell us his new medicine.
   a. someone who pretends to have special skills that he or she does not really have
   b. someone who has special skills or knowledge in a certain field

10. She bought her house for $100,000. She **made a killing** five years later when she sold it for $250,000.
    a. lost a lot of money
    b. earned a lot of money very easily

11. The country's most valuable products on the international **commodities market** are grapes and wheat.
    a. place where products can be traded, bought, or sold
    b. place where you can grow crops

You are going to read an article about the business of predicting the future. What do you want to find out about this topic? Write two questions you would like the article to answer.

1. _____

2. _____

AS YOU READ

As you read the article by William Sherden based on his book *The Fortune Sellers*, verify the predictions you wrote in Before You Read, Exercise D.

The Fortune Sellers
The Need to Know the Future

William Sherden

1   What will the future bring? The desire to know the future is a deep, psychological human need. Throughout history, people have devised ways to predict the future. Our earliest written records from 5,000 years ago show that forecasting was widely practiced in the ancient world. Thousands of years ago, people made predictions about the future by looking for patterns and clues in everything from the shape of sticks to the position of stars. Today, people are still trying to predict the future, but many of them base their predictions on scientific information.

The Business of Predicting

2   Lots of people are willing to pay to get information about the future. One reason they pay to know what is going to happen in the future is because of the money the knowledge can bring. For example, it would be a **piece of cake** to make a million dollars in the **stock market** if you knew in advance whether the economy was going to **expand** or **contract** at a certain time or which new technologies were going to become successful. You could **make a killing** in the **commodities market** if you could predict the climate for next year's growing season, which would give you a good idea about which crops would do well.

3   In fact, the practice of making predictions has become a huge business. It is a multibillion-dollar industry that employs hundreds of thousands of people. These people are not <u>merely</u> fortune-tellers, they are fortune sellers who offer us a product we're eager to buy: the future. They work in all kinds of professions from science and banking to astrology. Among the scientifically oriented professionals are

investment advisers who predict tomorrow's **hottest** stock, meteorologists who give us our daily weather forecasts, and seismologists who predict earthquakes. The more unscientific amateurs include astrologers who base predictions on the movement of stars and fortune-tellers who read tea leaves or palms to predict the future. As a result of their work, we are exposed daily to forecasts of the weather, economy, stock market, politics, society, and even love.

Failures of the Predictions Industry

4   Each year the prediction industry **showers** us with billions of dollars' worth of information. Unfortunately, most of the information is incorrect. The forecasting **accuracy** for all types of experts is poor. The truth is that the predictions of scientifically oriented professionals are no better than the predictions of astrologers and fortune-tellers. In fact, the experts whose advice we pay so much for often fail to predict the major events that shape our world. Recent events that caught the forecasters by total surprise include the entry of women into the workforce in <u>massive</u> numbers; the fall of communist Eastern Europe; the "baby boom" when so many babies were born after World War II and the later "baby bust" when the birth rate slowed; the stock market crash of 1929 and other, more recent changes in financial markets; the devastating floods in California; and the use of lasers to transmit telephone messages.

The Unknowable Future

5   Despite all the advances in science and technology that are available, experts are not getting any better at prediction. In some respects, we are hardly better off than the ancient Romans or Greeks, who used the bones and organs of dead animals to make decisions about the future. Today the prediction industry attracts some of the best and **brightest** minds. It also uses some of the latest technology. How then can the experts get it so wrong? The answer to that question is that the experts are trying to do the impossible. Recent developments in science show that the future is basically unpredictable. This finding applies to our economy, the stock market, commodity prices, the weather, human population, and many other things. There are no clear historical paths to the future. History does not repeat itself. The future remains mostly unknowable.

6   The fact that we cannot predict the future has been known to better minds for many years. Winston Churchill complained that the future was one damn thing after another. Benjamin Franklin said that the only things certain in life are death and taxes. Charles Richter, the inventor of the Richter scale, which measures earthquakes, said, "Only fools, liars, and **charlatans** predict earthquakes." That judgment can be applied to most other forecasts as well. The movements of tides and celestial objects, such as the planets, stars, and moons, are predictable long into the future, but they are the rare exceptions. Almost everything else that touches our lives is filled with uncertainty and becomes less predictable even though we try to look weeks, months, and years into the future.

AFTER YOU READ

Check Your Comprehension

A. Circle the letter of the answer that best completes each statement or answers the question.

1. Who would be most likely to give you information about which stocks to buy?
   a. A meteorologist
   b. An investment adviser
   c. A seismologist

2. The word <u>merely</u> in paragraph 3 means _____.
   a. just
   b. unfortunately
   c. young

3. The author refers to the use of lasers to transmit telephone messages as an example of _____.
   a. the impact of technology on communication
   b. a recent event that surprised forecasters
   c. recent improvements in the telecommunications industry

4. According to the article, investment advisors, meteorologists, and seismologists _____.
   a. make predictions that are usually correct
   b. are scientifically oriented professionals
   c. often complain about the future

5. Which statement would the author be most likely to agree with?
   a. Ancient cultures were better at making predictions than we are today.
   b. Few things in life are predictable.
   c. It is a good idea to base an investment of a lot of money on economic predictions.

6. The author uses Winston Churchill, Benjamin Franklin, and Charles Richter as examples of people _____.
   a. who made important inventions
   b. whose ideas he disagrees with
   c. who understood that the future was unpredictable

7. The terms *baby boom* and *baby bust* have _____.
   a. negative meanings
   b. opposite meanings
   c. similar meanings

8. You can infer that the author believes that the experts _____.
   a. can try harder to be more accurate
   b. should charge higher prices
   c. can't improve their predictions

9. According to the article, which of the following can be predicted with some accuracy?
   a. The movement of the tides
   b. The agricultural commodities market
   c. The weather

10. The word <u>massive</u> in paragraph 4 means
    a. small
    b. huge
    c. questionable

Sharpen Your Vocabulary Skills

UNDERSTANDING COMPOUND WORDS

 Compound words are words that are made of two or more separate words. For example, the word *toothache* is a compound word. It is made of the two words *tooth* and *ache*. If you know the meanings of these two words, you can guess what *toothache* means. It is often easier to begin analyzing the meaning of a compound word if you begin with the second word. For example, a *toothache* is an ache or pain in your tooth.

A. Look at each of the following compound words from the articles in this chapter. Write a definition of each word.

1. fingernail _____

2. teacup _____

3. newspaper _____

4. website _____

5. self-discovery _____

6. fortune-teller _____

7. workforce _____

8. earthquake _____

B. Write four sentences that use the words. Try to use two compound words in each sentence.

_____

_____

_____

_____

Evaluate Your Ideas

1. Now that you have read the article, reread the statements in the Evaluate the Statements Chart on page 130 and mark Agree or Disagree for each one in the After You Read column.

2. Talk to a partner about why any of your new responses differed from the ones you made before you read the article.

3. Find and discuss the specific information in the article that supports each of your opinions.

Share Your Thoughts

Work in small groups to discuss these questions.

1. Do you agree with Winston Churchill's complaint that the future is one damn thing after another? What about Benjamin Franklin's idea that the only things certain in life are death and taxes?

2. The article mentioned several events that people didn't predict would happen (the entry of women into the workforce in massive numbers; the fall of communist Eastern Europe; the "baby boom" after World War II; the stock market crash of 1929; recent changes in financial markets; the devastating floods in California; the use of lasers to transmit telephone messages). What do you know about any of these events? What other events can you think of that were not predicted?

3. Would you like to work in the predictions industry? Why or why not? If yes, which field would you like to work in?

4. The author concludes the article with these thoughts: "There are no clear historical paths to the future. History does not repeat itself. The future remains mostly unknowable." Do you agree with these conclusions? Why or why not? Do you think history repeats itself? Give some examples to support your opinion.

Explore the Web

What is your Zodiac sign? There are many sites on the Internet that give daily or weekly horoscopes. Use the Internet to look up your horoscope for today or this week. If you don't know your sign, use the following chart to find the sign that matches your birthdate. Write your horoscope after your Zodiac sign. Share it with a small group and discuss whether you think it is accurate or not.

Signs of the Zodiac and Their Dates	My Horoscope
Aries March 21 to April 20	
Taurus April 21 to May 20	
Gemini May 21 to June 21	
Cancer June 22 to July 22	
Leo July 23 to August 22	
Virgo August 23 to September 22	
Libra September 23 to October 22	
Scorpio October 23 to November 22	
Sagittarius November 23 to December 21	
Capricorn December 22 to January 20	
Aquarius January 21 to February 19	
Pisces February 20 to March 20	

Go Beyond the Text

Have you ever been to a restaurant that serves fortune cookies? Inside a fortune cookie there is a slip of paper with a future prediction or a message of advice. Have you ever read your fortune from a fortune cookie? Cut out a small slip of paper and write a "fortune" on it. Fold up your paper and exchange fortunes with another student.

CHAPTER 7

Distinguish Fact from Opinion

Guernica by Pablo Picasso

About the Artist

Pablo Picasso was born in 1881 in Malaga, Spain, but he lived in France from 1904 until his death in 1973. He is considered one of the greatest and most influential figures in twentieth century art. An inspired painter, he is also known for his ability in ceramics, drawing, prints, and sculpture. Picasso's father was an artist and an art teacher who recognized and nurtured his son's extraordinary talent starting at a very young age. Part of what made Picasso so great was his ability to respond so easily to change and work so well in different media and styles. As an artist, he was always experimenting and looking for new techniques. Picasso painted Guernica in 1937 for the Pavilion of the Spanish Republic at the Paris International Exposition.

Look at Picasso's painting. Work with a partner and talk about what you see in the painting.

1. What is the painting about? Describe what you see.

   _____

   _____

   _____

2. How do you think Picasso felt about war? What images did he use to support his opinion?

   _____

   _____

   _____

In this painting, Picasso was expressing his opinion about the brutality of war. Like artists, writers often express their own opinions.

Sharpen Your Reading Skills

DISTINGUISHING FACT FROM OPINION

Learning to distinguish between facts and opinions is a valuable skill. **Facts** are statements that can be proven to be true. **Opinions** are statements that describe someone's feelings or beliefs about a topic. The ability to distinguish between facts and opinions will help you to make judgments about what you read.

Consider this statement:

- Pablo Picasso is the best artist of the twentieth century.

Do you agree or disagree with the statement? ☐ Agree ☐ Disagree

It is possible to agree or disagree with the statement because it is an opinion. You cannot prove whether Picasso is the best artist of the twentieth century or not. Opinions are beliefs that cannot be proven.

Now consider this statement:

- Pablo Picasso was born in Malaga, Spain, on October 25, 1881.

You can't agree or disagree with this statement because it is a fact. You can look at records such as a birth certificate to see exactly where and when Picasso was born. Facts can be checked. They can be observed, counted, and measured. Unlike opinions, facts can be proven to be true.

Although it is a very important skill, it is not always easy to recognize the difference between a fact and an opinion. Here are some tips.

1. Opinions often use value adjectives such as

brilliant	terrible	disgusting	beautiful	original
excellent	wonderful	trustworthy	bad	spectacular
fair	effective	lovely	appropriate	disappointing
innovative	great	ugly	kind	magnificent

- Pablo Picasso's style was effective and original.

2. Opinions often use words that show comparison, such as

more	most	less	least
better	best	stronger	strongest

- Pablo Picasso was more innovative and willing to take risks than the other painters of his time.

3. Be aware that much of what you read in newspapers, essays, or magazines is a combination of facts and the opinions of the author.

- Ali deservedly won the essay contest two years in a row.

This sentence does two things. It states the fact that Ali won the contest two years in a row, and it also expresses the author's opinion by saying that Ali "deservedly" won the contest.

4. Authors sometimes disguise their opinions as facts to make their argument seem more believable.

- In fact, boys are better at math than girls.
- The fact of the matter is that Ms. Chen's experience makes her a superior candidate.
- The truth is that our schools have never been in such bad shape.

Authors do not always use expressions such as "truly," "in fact," "the fact of the matter," and "as a matter of fact" to introduce facts. Sometimes they use them to make their opinions seem like facts. These statements are the writer's point of view, although they may appear to be facts. The words "better" "superior candidate," and "bad shape" show that they are opinions.

 As you read, try to distinguish between facts and opinions. Remember that opinions can be argued, facts cannot. Facts can be proved, opinions cannot.

Read the article and do the exercise on page 142.

Guernica

A Masterpiece of Modern Art

1   Although Pablo Picasso produced more than 50,000 works, *Guernica* is justifiably considered one of his greatest works. In fact, it is one of the masterpieces of modern art. In 1937 Picasso was commissioned by the Spanish Republican government to paint a picture to decorate the Spanish Pavilion at the World's Fair in Paris. For this he created *Guernica,* a painting depicting the bombing of the Spanish town of Guernica during the Spanish Civil War. The painting is large—25 feet wide and 11 feet high—and Picasso painted it in just one month. *Guernica* is the most powerful condemnation of the horrors of war ever created. Corpses and dying figures fill the foreground of the painting. There is a woman with a dead child on the left, a crying woman and a figure falling through a burning building on the right. In the center you can see the most effective image, a dead warrior with a broken sword.

2   Picasso effectively used several techniques to convey a message and emphasize a sense of shock, fear, and confusion. For example, he limited his use of color to black, white, and gray. He did so to evoke feelings of sadness and hopelessness and to show the seriousness of the subject. In addition, he distorted and exaggerated the figures in the painting. This way he ensured that the viewer felt the violence and utter despair of war. He used depictions of human and animal body parts to express pain and inhumanity. In *Guernica,* Picasso painted powerful images to show us the agony of war. He used the tools he was best at using to make a statement about the disasters that war creates. It is a hard painting to look at, but it is also a wonderful one. Looking at a painting like this today, we are immediately reminded of the dangers of war.

3   For many years, from 1939 until 1981, *Guernica* was on extended loan to New York City's Museum of Modern Art. In 1981 it was returned to Spain, where it was displayed in Madrid's Prado Museum. In 1992, *Guernica* was moved to the Reina Sofia Art Center, Spain's national museum of modern art.

Indicate whether each of the following statements from the article is a fact, an opinion, or a combination of fact and opinion. Write F, O, or F + O on the line.

Example

F + O   Although Pablo Picasso produced more than 50,000 works, *Guernica* is justifiably considered one of his greatest works.

_____ **1.** The painting is large—25 feet wide and 11 feet high—and Picasso painted it in just one month.

_____ **2.** In fact, it is one of the masterpieces of modern art.

_____ **3.** *Guernica* is the most powerful condemnation ever created of the horrors of war.

_____ **4.** In 1937, Picasso was commissioned by the Spanish Republican government to paint a picture to decorate the Spanish Pavilion at the World's Fair in Paris.

_____ **5.** For example, he limited his use of color to black, white, and gray.

_____ **6.** It is a hard painting to look at, but it is also a wonderful one.

_____ **7.** Picasso effectively used several techniques to convey a message and emphasize a sense of shock, fear, and confusion.

_____ **8.** In 1992, *Guernica* was moved to the Reina Sofia Art Center, Spain's national museum of modern art.

_____ **9.** In the center you can see the most effective image, a dead warrior with a broken sword.

_____ **10.** For many years, from 1939 until 1981, *Guernica* was on extended loan to New York City's Museum of Modern Art.

Be an Active Reader

READING 1: Seattle

BEFORE YOU READ

Activate Your Background Knowledge

A. Discuss these questions with a partner.

1. Have you ever been to the northwestern part of the United States? If yes, where? What were your impressions of it?

2. What is the climate like in your city? What is your favorite kind of climate? Why?

3. Have you ever heard of the companies Starbucks (coffee), Microsoft, and Amazon.com? What do you know about them? Are there any big companies located in your part of the country? What are they?

4. What do you know about the history of the area where you live? How and when was it founded?

Preview and Predict

B. Read the title, subtitle, and headings of the article on pages 145–147. Look at the map and pictures and read the caption. Can you guess what the article will tell you about the city of Seattle, Washington? Think of several topics that might be discussed in the article.

1. _____
2. _____
3. _____
4. _____

Preview the Vocabulary

C. The words in the box are boldfaced in the article. Complete the Vocabulary Chart with words from the box. If necessary, use your dictionary.

Words to Watch

settlers	headquarters	spectacular
progressive	thriving	hospitable
cosmopolitan	reputation	treaty
eloquently	high-tech	

Vocabulary Chart	
Word	**Definition**
	consisting of people from many different parts of the world
	supporting new or modern ideas
	friendly, welcoming, and generous to visitors
	a building or office that is the center of a large organization
	the opinion that people have of someone or something because of what has happened in the past
	using the most modern information, machines, and so on
	very successful
	people who go to live in a new place, usually where there were few people before
	clearly; expressing your ideas, opinions, or feelings so that they influence other people
	very impressive or exciting
	a formal written agreement between two or more countries

Set a Purpose

You are going to read an article about the city of Seattle. What do you want to find out about this city? Write two questions you would like the article to answer.

1. _____

2. _____

Seattle
A City with a View and Worth Viewing

Geography and Climate

1   Seattle, a city located in Washington, the state farthest north and west in the contiguous United States*, is well known for its magnificent scenery. The city is surrounded by beautiful landscapes and water. Seattle is built on hills facing two lakes and Puget Sound, a body of water that leads to the Pacific Ocean. From the hills of Seattle there are **spectacular** views of snow-covered mountains. The Olympic and Cascade mountain ranges surround Seattle, and there is a view of nearby Mount Rainier, an active volcano over 14,000 feet high that is covered with ice and snow.

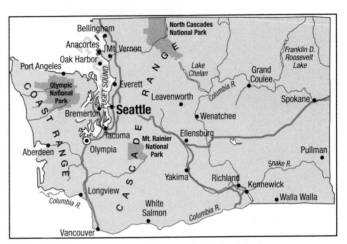

Seattle is located near lakes and mountains in Washington.

2   Although the state of Washington borders Canada to the north, the climate of Seattle is fairly mild since it is near the ocean. The winter temperatures are not very cold, falling below freezing only a few days per year. However, the sky is often cloudy, and Seattle has a **reputation** as a city that gets little sunshine. In fact, it gets less rain than several other major American cities.

The Founding of Seattle

3   Seattle was named after a Native American Indian chief who was friendly and **hospitable**. He and his people, the Suquamish, helped the first American **settlers** who moved to the Washington area in the second half of the nineteenth century. Chief Seattle signed a peace **treaty** with the U.S. government in 1854 that allowed U.S. citizens to settle in the area. In signing the treaty, Chief Seattle hoped to avoid the fighting that had occurred in other parts of the country when settlers moved into Native American lands. In a famous speech, Chief Seattle spoke out **eloquently**

Seattle is in the northwestern part of the United States.

against violence and encouraged the new American settlers to respect the land and the

(continued)

*__Contiguous United States:__ The U.S., excluding Alaska and Hawaii.

Among Seattle's beautiful views are those of Mount Rainier, a glacier-capped volcano.

rights of Native Americans. He declared, "This we know: The earth does not belong to man; man belongs to the earth. This we know. All things are connected like the blood which unites one family. All things are connected."

4   The Suquamish had lived in the Washington area for many generations, and they were able to live peacefully with the new settlers when they arrived. The city of Seattle was founded in 1869. The population grew very quickly after the Alaskan gold rush, which started in 1897. Thousands of people passed through the state of Washington on their way to look for gold in Alaska. Many stayed to develop the region, and Seattle became a growing city. Today the population of Seattle is close to 600,000.

Home to Contemporary Business

5   Although it is younger than most other major American cities, Seattle has become an important center of trade and industry and is home to some of America's leading companies.

Seattle is a port city that is a key center for trade with Canada, Mexico, Europe, and many Asian countries. Because of its location in the western part of the United States near the Pacific Ocean, it is sometimes called the "Gateway to Asia." For many years, Seattle has been a prosperous city with major industries such as aerospace, which produces airplanes and spacecraft. In recent years, the city has become famous as the center of some major contemporary corporations. Seattle is the home and **headquarters** of Starbucks, a leading coffee company. The first Starbucks café

Starbucks opened its first store in 1971 in downtown Seattle.

opened in Seattle in 1971, and the business has expanded to thousands of locations around the world. Another important industry for Seattle is computer software, for the giant company Microsoft has its headquarters near Seattle. In addition, the founder of Amazon.com, the online company, moved to Seattle to create his new business and establish its headquarters there. Today Seattle is a wonderful **cosmopolitan** city with a **thriving** economy.

A Popular Choice of Residence

6   Seattle has a mild climate, successful industries, and great natural beauty, and it is well known for the high level of its education and cultural attractions. One of the major architectural sites in the city is a beautiful, large public library, which opened in 2004. Designed by a prominent Dutch architect, the library has a contemporary design and many **high-tech** features. Seattle has earned a reputation as a **progressive** city. In several surveys, Americans have chosen Seattle as one of the most desirable places to live in the United States.

AFTER YOU READ

Check Your Comprehension

A. True or false? Write T (True) or F (False) next to each of the following statements. If a statement is false, rewrite it to make it true.

_____ 1. Seattle developed as a city because of the Alaskan gold rush.

_____ 2. Seattle is considered a desirable place to live for several reasons.

_____ 3. Seattle is often cloudy but doesn't get much rain.

_____ 4. Seattle is home to most of America's leading companies.

_____ 5. Chief Seattle wanted people to respect the land and each other.

_____ 6. Aerospace is a recent industry in Seattle.

_____ 7. The Suquamish did not get along well with the new settlers.

_____ 8. Seattle is sometimes called the "Gateway to Asia" because it is near the Pacific Ocean.

_____ 9. Chief Seattle supported violence and revenge.

Distinguish Fact from Opinion

B. Indicate whether each of the following statements from the article is a fact, an opinion, or a combination of fact and opinion. Write F, O, or F + O on the line.

_____ 1. Seattle has spectacular views of snow-covered mountains.

_____ 2. The Olympic and Cascade mountain ranges surround Seattle, and there is a view of nearby Mount Rainier, an active volcano over 14,000 feet high that is covered with ice and snow.

_____ 3. Chief Seattle signed a peace treaty with the U.S. government in 1854 that allowed U.S. citizens to settle in the Washington area.

_____ 4. In a famous speech, Chief Seattle spoke out eloquently against violence and revenge and encouraged the new American settlers to respect the land and the rights of Native Americans.

(continued)

_____ **5.** Today the population of Seattle is close to 600,000.

_____ **6.** The first Starbucks café opened in Seattle in 1971, and the business has expanded to thousands of locations around the world.

_____ **7.** Seattle was named after a Native American Indian chief who was friendly and hospitable.

_____ **8.** One of the major architectural sites in the city is a beautiful, large public library, which opened in 2004.

_____ **9.** Today Seattle is a wonderfully cosmopolitan city with a thriving economy.

Test Your Vocabulary

C. Complete each of the sentences that follow with a word from the box. Be sure to use the correct form of the word.

settlers	headquarters	spectacular	progressive
thriving	hospitable	cosmopolitan	reputation
treaty	eloquently	high-tech	

1. After the war, the two countries signed a peace _____.

2. Tokyo is a city with many companies and a _____ economy.

3. Hong Kong is a _____ city where you can meet people from all over the world.

4. Dr. Zahi Hawass has earned a _____ as an excellent archaeologist and Egyptologist.

5. Lakshmi works in a _____ communications company with the most advanced equipment.

6. The company's _____ are in Seoul, but there are smaller offices in cities throughout Asia.

7. Paula's grandmother has very traditional ideas and often criticizes Paula for her _____ attitude.

8. The local people were very _____ to us when we visited.

9. She spoke _____ about the importance of early childhood education.

10. The early _____ of the American West faced many challenges.

11. We took lots of pictures of the _____ views from the top of the mountain.

Sum It Up

Write a one-paragraph summary of "Seattle." Remember to include only main ideas from the article in your summary.

_____

_____

_____

_____

Share Your Thoughts

A. Work with a small group and discuss these questions.

1. Have you ever visited Seattle? If not, would you like to?

2. Why do you think Seattle is the home and headquarters of so many big companies?

3. Would you like to live in a city like Seattle? Give some reasons to support your answer.

4. What do you think Chief Seattle meant when he said, "This we know: The earth does not belong to man; man belongs to the earth. This we know. All things are connected like the blood which unites one family. All things are connected." Do you agree with him? Why or why not?

B. Choose one of the questions in Exercise A and write a paragraph about it.

_____

_____

_____

_____

READING 2: The Best Cities in the United States

BEFORE YOU READ

You have just read an article about a city that many Americans have chosen in surveys as one of the most desirable places to live in the United States. Now you are going to read an article that discusses how surveys determine which cities are considered the most desirable places to live.

Activate Your Background Knowledge

A. What factors are important to you about where you live? Complete the chart. Then compare and discuss responses with a partner.

Factors in Choosing a Place to Live			
Factors	Very Important	Somewhat Important	Not at All Important
Climate			
Variety of cultural institutions (museums, art galleries, theaters, and so on)			
Cost of living			
Housing prices			
Crime rates			
Quality of hospitals and health care			
Amount of pollution			
Quality of schools			
Size			
Employment opportunities			

Preview and Predict

B. Read the title and headings of the article on pages 152–153. Think of several topics that might be discussed in the article.

1. _____

2. _____

3. _____

4. _____

C. The words and phrases in the box are boldfaced in the article. Complete the Vocabulary Chart with words from the box. If necessary, use your dictionary.

Words to Watch

criteria	facilities	category
claim	priority	break down
compile	relocate	survey

Vocabulary Chart	
Word	**Definition**
	a group of people or things that have the same qualities
	to make a book, list, or record using different pieces of information
	places or buildings used for a particular purpose
	to state that something is true, even if it has not been proved
	a set of questions that you ask a large number of people to find out about their opinions and behavior
	the thing you think is most important
	to move to a new place
	facts or standards used to help you judge or decide something
	to make something, such as a job, report, or plan, simpler by dividing it into parts

Set a Purpose

You are going to read an article about how cities are rated. Write several questions you would like the article to answer.

_____

_____

The Best Cities in the United States

1   Every year there are new lists of the top ten cities to live in, as rated by different organizations such as *Money Magazine* and *Forbes*. Rarely, though, do the same cities appear at the top of each **survey**. On one list, San Francisco might be the number one city in the United States, while Seattle might top the list in another survey. Within the United States, cities such as Portland, Oregon; Denver, Colorado; and Pittsburgh, Pennsylvania, have appeared on lists of best cities to live in.

Factors in Determining the Ranking

2   What makes a city the "best"? Each organization uses different **criteria** to determine the ranking. Factors such as climate, cost of living, housing prices, and crime rates are often considered. In addition, some surveys consider health care **facilities** and levels of air pollution. Employment opportunities and predictions for future job growth are also key elements in evaluating places to live. Las Vegas, Nevada, and Austin, Texas, are two cities that rank high in job opportunities. An important factor in many surveys is the variety of cultural institutions such as museums, art galleries, and theaters and the number of musicians and other artists. Cities such as New York and Washington, D.C., often appear in top ten lists because of this **category**. The quality of schools and universities is another consideration in some surveys. Not surprisingly, Ann Arbor, Michigan; Madison, Wisconsin; and Boston, Massachusetts, are ranked high in such surveys.

Considering the Factors

3   Many cities can **claim** to be ranked in the top ten since there are numerous lists. Besides looking at popular lists to see which cities are highly rated, it is important to examine the factors used in determining the ratings and evaluate for oneself which factors should have highest **priority**. After all, what is most important to some people might not be as important to others. One person might be most interested in education levels, health care facilities, and low housing costs, while another might value cultural institutions and job opportunities. Some organizations offer a detailed analysis of their evaluation methods in determining the rankings and **break down** the ratings into several categories. For example, they rank by geographical location, such as best cities in the East, West, or Central United States, and by size, such as best large, medium, and small cities. Others **compile** lists with categories such as best cities for single people or best cities for families.

Finding Your Dream City

4   For anyone trying to decide where to **relocate**, plenty of information is available about each city's resources and statistics. Numerous websites provide excellent

information about American cities. At some sites, you can even find out which cities are the most and least stressful in the United States. If you're dreaming of living somewhere else, a number of helpful surveys can assist you in finding your ideal city. Before you make a decision about where to live, take a look at some of them.

AFTER YOU READ

Check Your Comprehension

A. Circle the letter of the word or phrase that best completes each sentence or answers the question.

1. Climate, cost of living, and housing prices are examples of _____.
   a. the most important factors to consider when choosing a place to live
   b. some of the factors an organization might use to determine the ranking of cities
   c. factors that make San Francisco an attractive city

2. Las Vegas, Nevada, and Austin, Texas, _____.
   a. are rarely ranked highly
   b. rank high for their cultural institutions
   c. rate highly in the job opportunity category

3. According to the article, what city often ranks high for the quality of its schools and universities?
   a. Ann Arbor, Michigan
   b. Las Vegas, Nevada
   c. Pittsburgh, Pennsylvania

4. From the article, you can infer that the author _____.
   a. thinks the quality of education is high in Ann Arbor, Madison, and Boston
   b. is surprised that Ann Arbor, Madison, and Boston rank high in the education category
   c. went to school in Ann Arbor, Madison, or Boston

5. Why is it possible for many cities to claim to be ranked in the top ten?
   a. Because there are so many cities in the United States
   b. Because there are many different lists
   c. Because no one pays much attention to the rankings

6. The author gives _____ examples of the best cities for single people.
   a. no
   b. several
   c. many

7. In paragraph 2, the word *key* is closest in meaning to _____.
   a. insignificant
   b. important
   c. irrelevant

8. In paragraph 3, the word *besides* is closest in meaning to _____.
   a. in addition to
   b. next to
   c. however

Distinguish Fact from Opinion

B. Indicate whether each of the following statements from the article is a fact, an opinion, or a combination of fact and opinion. Write F, O, or F + O on the line.

_____ 1. Every year there are new lists of the top ten cities to live in, as rated by different organizations such as *Money Magazine* and *Forbes*.

_____ 2. Some organizations offer a detailed analysis of their evaluation methods in determining the rankings and break down the ratings into several categories.

_____ 3. Numerous websites provide excellent information about American cities.

_____ 4. Others compile lists with categories such as best cities for single people or best cities for families.

_____ 5. Not surprisingly, Ann Arbor, Michigan; Madison, Wisconsin; and Boston, Massachusetts, are ranked high in such surveys.

_____ 6. If you're dreaming of living somewhere else, a number of helpful surveys can assist you in finding your ideal city.

Sharpen Your Vocabulary Skills

LEARNING COLLOCATIONS

Collocations are words that often appear together. For example, in this chapter you learned the word *treaty*. *Treaty* often appears with the word *peace*, and the phrase *peace treaty* is a common collocation. When you learn a language it is helpful to notice which words often go together to form collocations.

One of the most common types of collocations is the adjective + noun combination. Here are some examples of adjective + noun collocations from this chapter:

spectacular views

thriving economy

high-tech features

Another common type of collocation is the verb + noun combination. For example, the noun *treaty* also appears with the verb *sign*, and the phrase *sign a treaty* is a common collocation. Here are some examples of verb + noun collocations from this chapter:

do the exercise

make a decision, **make** a statement

take a look
earn a reputation
sign a peace treaty

PRACTICE IN COLLOCATIONS

A. Complete each sentence with a word from the box.

| spectacular   thriving   high-tech |

1. Look at that _____ sunset.

2. The new laboratory has a lot of _____ equipment.

3. My friends owns a _____ business that employs hundreds of people.

4. Did you notice the _____ scenery along the river?

5. We work in a _____ industry with the most advanced communications systems.

6. Let's take a picture of that _____ rainbow.

7. Their army has a _____ weapons system.

B. Complete each sentence with the best word from the box. Be sure to use the correct form of the word.

| do   make   take   earn   sign |

1. Please _____ me a favor.

2. Don't forget to _____ the check.

3. You need to _____ the lease before you move into the apartment.

4. After he became a citizen, he _____ the right to vote in national elections.

5. If you are tired, you should _____ a rest.

6. It's time for you to _____ a decision about whether you are going to _____ the job.

7. I can't go to the movies; I need to _____ my homework.

8. My car is _____ a strange noise.

9. When do you plan to _____ the shopping?

10. He _____ a living by selling his paintings.

TIP It is often difficult to know which words go together to form collocations. To help you learn common collocations, make a list of collocations that you come across while reading and keep them in your notebook.

Share Your Thoughts

A. Work in small groups to discuss these questions.

1. What is your favorite city? Why?

2. What is your least favorite city? Why?

3. If you could live anywhere, where would you choose? What factors influenced your decision?

4. On a scale of 1 (excellent) to 5 (poor), how would you rank the area where you live?

B. Choose one of the questions in Exercise A and write a paragraph about it.

_____

_____

_____

_____

Explore the Web

What cities do you think are the most expensive and least expensive in the world to live in? This year, CNN and *Money Magazine* conducted a survey to find out. Use the Internet to find the five cities in the world that are the most expensive to live in and the five that are the least expensive.

World's Five Most Expensive Cities	World's Five Least Expensive Cities

Go Beyond the Text

Look at the chart Factors in Choosing a Place to Live on page 150. Use the chart to take a survey of some of your friends and family. Choose ten people to survey. Compile the results and fill in the following chart. Share the results of your survey with your classmates.

Factors in Choosing a Place to Live	
_____ % said climate was very important.	_____ % said amount of pollution was very important.
_____ % said climate was somewhat important.	_____ % said amount of pollution was somewhat important.
_____ % said climate was not important.	_____ % said amount of pollution was not important.
_____ % said the variety of cultural institutions was very important.	_____ % said size was very important.
_____ % said the variety of cultural institutions was somewhat important.	_____ % said size was somewhat important.
_____ % said the variety of cultural institutions was not important.	_____ % said size was not important.
_____ % said housing prices were very important.	_____ % said quality of schools was very important.
_____ % said housing prices were somewhat important.	_____ % said quality of schools was somewhat important.
_____ % said housing prices were not important.	_____ % said quality of schools was not important.
_____ % said crime rates were very important.	_____ % said cost of living was very important.
_____ % said crime rates were somewhat important.	_____ % said cost of living was somewhat important.
_____ % said crime rates were not important.	_____ % said cost of living was not important.
_____ % said quality of hospitals and health care was very important.	_____ % said employment opportunities were very important.
_____ % said quality of hospitals and health care was somewhat important.	_____ % said employment opportunities were somewhat important.
_____ % said quality of hospitals and health care was not important.	_____ % said employment opportunities were not important.

CHAPTER 8

Understand the Author's Purpose and Tone

Great Wave off Kanagawa by Katsushika Hokusai

About the Artist

Katsushika Hokusai (1760–1849) was a Japanese painter and printmaker who was completely devoted to his work. His most famous works are *The Thirty-six Views of Mount Fuji,* produced in 1827. During his life, Hokusai produced tens of thousands of paintings, prints, and illustrations. His images were usually taken from the countryside, people, and legends of Japan. Hokusai's prints influenced many western artists, including van Gogh, Monet, Degas, and Toulouse-Lautrec. The Hokusai picture is one of many that deal with the theme of water and Mount Fuji, the cone-shaped volcano with a snow-covered peak that is beautiful yet capable of devastating destruction.

Look carefully at the picture by Katsushika Hokusai on page 158 and discuss the following questions with a partner.

1. What is the picture about?

   _____

   _____

2. How do you think Hokusai felt about nature?

   _____

   _____

   _____

3. Find the fishing boats out on the waves. These small boats create a sense of the smallness of man compared to the huge power of nature. In this picture, Hokusai expresses his philosophy that nature, not man, controls the world. This was his purpose in creating this picture. Do you agree with Hokusai's view? Why or why not?

   _____

   _____

   _____

> *Just as artists create for a purpose, authors create with a purpose in mind. They have a clear purpose when they write.*

Sharpen Your Reading Skills

UNDERSTANDING THE AUTHOR'S PURPOSE

Identifying an author's purpose will help you understand and appreciate what you read. Some of the most common purposes for writing are **to inform**, **to entertain**, and **to persuade**.

Read these examples of the three most common purposes for writing.

1. Purpose: To inform readers about something

   For most of history, shoes have been used to symbolize social status, power, and wealth. The material used to make shoes, the amount of decoration, and the color and height of shoes all served to indicate the importance and wealth of the people who wore the shoes. During some periods in history, high heels expressed the idea of a life of great leisure and luxury. For example, from the 1300s to the 1700s, some wealthy women in Europe wore shoes so high that they couldn't walk without support.

2. Purpose: To entertain readers

Roger Storm was a qualified meteorologist who worked for a local TV news program. Everybody liked Roger, but he had a terrible weather-forecasting record. He became the target of jokes when a newspaper began keeping a record of his predictions and showed that he'd been wrong almost 300 times in one year. It got to the point where no one in the viewing audience believed any of his predictions. Eventually, all his forecasting mistakes got him fired. He moved to a different city in another part of the country and applied for a job at one of the local TV stations. When he was asked the reason for leaving his previous job, Roger said, "The climate didn't agree with me."

3. Purpose: To persuade or convince readers of something

The new shampoo Shine On by Colette Cosmetics will improve the texture of your hair in only two weeks. If you use this shampoo daily, your hair will be softer, silkier, and easier to manage. Best of all, it will be shinier and look healthier.

Keep in mind that the three purposes are not always mutually exclusive. Writers often accomplish several purposes at the same time. For example, an article may be amusing and also informative or persuasive. To understand and evaluate what you read, you need to consider the author's reason for writing.

PRACTICE IN IDENTIFYING PURPOSE

Read each of the following selections and decide whether the author's purpose is to entertain, to inform, or to persuade. Some selections may have more than one purpose.

1. Huge areas of tropical rain forests all around the world are being destroyed every year. The trees in the tropical rain forests are being cut down for their valuable wood and to clear land for farming and housing. In 1950, rain forests covered 14 percent of the world's land surface. Today, they cover only 6 percent. Rain forests are disappearing so fast that some scientists worry that they may vanish completely during this century. The world's rain forests are home to a great variety of insects and animals that will die as their habitat is destroyed. Many of the animals are unique to rain forests and are important to the world's natural balance. As the rain forests are destroyed and the animals die, the natural balance is also destroyed. In addition, many of the world's 250,000 different types of plants are found only in rain forests. Important drugs that can help people fight diseases come from these plants. As a result of the destruction of the world's rain forests, possible cures for diseases are being lost forever.

Purpose: _____

2.   **I Hate the Internet**

I'm sick of clicking here and there—
        I hate receiving bytes,
Waiting for images to load,
        and looking for Web sites.

Libraries are more my style—
        I like the old-fashioned way.
I mean what does "dot com" really mean?
        And who cares, anyway?

I really hate the icons,
        and the lingo created by nerds.
If you ask me what I think,
        navigating's for the birds.

Downloading is a drag,
        and surfing makes me sick—
Browsing's more fun in stores.
        At least I get what I pick.

When did the world become a web?
        When did home become a page?
Hotlists leave me really cold,
        but maybe it's just a stage.

Take a trip through cyberspace—
        With keyboard and modem in hand.
Netscape will try to guide you,
        but you never know where you'll land.

Purpose: _____

3.   As Tropical Storm Florence edges closer to Bermuda, the island is being placed
under a tropical storm warning. This means that tropical storm conditions are
expected within twenty-four hours. According to forecasters at the National
Hurricane Center in Miami, Bermuda should expect strong winds and pounding surf
by Friday evening. Here are some things to keep in mind as the storm approaches:
know the risk to your area, know your evacuation routes, find out where emergency
shelters are located, and make and follow a family disaster preparedness plan.

Purpose: _____

4.   To the Editor:

    I'm writing about the proposal to create a new housing development on the
open land at the corner of Concord and Goodwill roads. That land has provided a
beautiful, green entrance to our town since the town was founded over 200 years
ago. It is a scenic view that welcomes people to our town and shows visitors that

this is a town that cares about natural beauty, preserving our heritage, and traditional values. It is one of the few pieces of land in this town and the surrounding towns that has not been converted to building for profit. Those of us who live in this town are proud of that open land, but I wonder how much pride we can feel if we ruin our beautiful land for commercial use. If we don't take care of our land for future generations, who will? What it comes down to is a question of being mean or remaining green. Think about it.

Purpose: _____

Understanding the Author's Tone

Tone is the general feeling or attitude expressed in a work of art or a piece of writing. Artists use shades of color in their paintings to express their feelings about the subject. For example, in painting *Guernica*, Picasso used only the colors black, white, and gray to evoke feelings of sadness and hopelessness and to show the seriousness of the subject. In a similar way, authors use words to express their feelings in writing.

 To determine the tone of a piece of writing, you need to look at the author's choice of words. The author's words might express a variety of emotions, such as hope, optimism, bitterness, loneliness, happiness, nostalgia, frustration, anger, or sadness.

Example

Read the following paragraph.

I've given up on trying to lose weight. My bookshelves are crowded with diet books and my refrigerator is filled with diet foods. I never want to count another calorie as long as I live. I've tried every diet you can imagine and nothing works.

Consider how you think the author felt as she wrote the paragraph. What tone did she use? The words and phrases *given up*, *crowded*, and *never want to count* show **frustration**.

a. frustrated
b. hopeful
c. mysterious

Identify the tone of each passage. Circle the letter of the adjective that describes the tone.

1. I've been on one diet or another for about ten years now, ever since the clerk at the Viennese Pastry Shop applied all that weight directly to my hips. Last week

I started a new diet. I've lost a lot on my new diet now that I'm using ounces instead of pounds to measure the loss. So far I've lost 112 ounces!

a. bitter
b. critical
c. humorous

2. These days communication is so fast-paced that I can hardly keep up. What ever happened to the days of long conversations over a cup of coffee? I miss the days when people would take the time to write a letter. Now it's all messages left on cell phones or e-mails dashed off on a computer.

a. humorous
b. nostalgic
c. optimistic

3. E-mail is the best thing that ever happened to me. Now I can keep in touch with all my friends and family much more easily. In just a few minutes I can communicate with lots of people. The first thing I do every morning is turn on my computer to see who has e-mailed me!

a. enthusiastic
b. bitter
c. critical

4. Every morning when I get to work, my e-mail inbox is flooded with unwanted— and often offensive—messages. I'm so sick of messages offering me things I don't want, telling lies I don't believe, or asking for money I don't have. It's getting to the point that I hate turning on my computer and checking my e-mail.

a. cheerful
b. uncertain
c. angry

5. If I had any doubts about Maxwell's ability to be mayor, his performance in last night's debate dispelled them. I am convinced that he will be a strong and capable leader. Maxwell showed amazing strength and belief in his ideas. His answers were honest and his vision clear. Our city needs new leadership, and Maxwell has a plan that will work. He left no doubt that he can lead our city toward a better future.

a. optimistic
b. depressing
c. lighthearted

6. Do you like to get up early? I do not. I hate to get up early, and my definition of early is any time before 8 A.M. Last week, however, I had to get up at 4:45 A.M. to begin the three-day, 45-mile (60 kilometer) Kepler Walk into New Zealand's Southern Alps. What spectacular scenery! What a fantastic experience! What a thrill! Some things are worth getting up early for!

a. angry
b. happy
c. confused

TIP | To understand the tone of a passage, think about the author's choice of words. Ask yourself this question: "What emotions do the words express? Are they hopeful, pessimistic, serious, bitter, fearful, happy, angry, enthusiastic, or _____?"

Be an Active Reader

READING 1: Why the Sea Is Salty

BEFORE YOU READ

Activate Your Background Knowledge

A. Folktales are short, fictional stories that may be set in any time and place. Read the statements in the chart that follows. Do you agree or disagree with these statements? Check your response in the first two columns. You will check the last columns after you read.

Agree	Disagree	Evaluate the Statements	Agree	Disagree
		Folktales are a way of preserving a group's history.		
		Folktales often reflect the values and customs of the culture from which they come.		
		Folktales are found in cultures worldwide.		
		Stories and folktales began as an attempt to explain and understand the natural and spiritual worlds.		

B. Work with a partner. Discuss the statements and compare responses.

C. Talk about folktales in your culture. Do you remember your parents or grandparents telling you any folktales when you were a child?

Preview and Predict

D. Take a few minutes to preview the story on pages 166–168. Read the title of the story. Look at the pictures. What do you think the story will be about?

E. The words and phrases in the box are boldfaced in the story. Complete the Vocabulary Chart with words from the box. If necessary, use your dictionary.

Words to Watch

make up (one's) mind	(my) heart skipped a beat	chatted
come up with (something)	get something out of (one's) mind	lavish
palace	pond	ministers

Vocabulary Chart	
Word	**Definition**
	politicians in charge of government departments
	to be suddenly very frightened, surprised, or excited
	to decide something or become very determined to do something
	talked in a friendly and informal way
	very generous and often expensive
	a small body of fresh water that is smaller than a lake
	a large house where a king or queen officially lives
	to think of an idea, plan, or reply
	to forget about something on purpose

Set a Purpose

You are going to read a folktale about a thief who stole a hand mill that had magic powers. Write several questions you would like the story to answer.

_____

_____

In Chapter 1 you learned about the importance of making predictions **before** you read. You can also use this strategy **while** you are reading. As you read the following story, make predictions about what you think will happen in the next part of the story.

Why the Sea Is Salty

1   Hundreds of years ago there was a king who had a very unusual hand mill. It looked like any other hand mill, but it had special powers. All one had to do was say what one wanted and turn the mill, and out would come what had been requested. If gold was requested, gold would come out. If rice was requested, rice would come out. Whatever was requested, the small hand mill would produce it.

2   A thief **made up his mind** to steal the magical hand mill because once he had heard of it, he couldn't **get it out of his mind.** For

When the king wishes for gold and turns the magical hand mill, gold comes out.

days and days he thought about how to steal it, but he could not **come up with** a plan.

Make a prediction. What do you think happens next?

_____

3   Then one day he dressed up like a scholar and visited a court official who had access to the royal **palace**. They **chatted** about this and that and finally the thief said, "I heard that the King buried his strange hand mill in the ground because he doesn't trust his **ministers.**"

4   "What's that? The King doesn't trust his ministers? Where did you hear such talk?"

5   "That's what they say in the countryside," said the thief, happy he had sparked the man's interest. "They say the King dug a deep hole and buried the hand mill because he is afraid that someone will steal it."

6   "That's nonsense!" said the official. "The King's hand mill is beside the lotus* **pond** in the inner court."

7   "Oh, is that so?" said the thief, trying to control his excitement.

8   "No one would dare try to steal the King's hand mill," said the official. "Who

*lotus: a plant with large flat leaves that floats on water

would even think of trying when the thing is lying right beside the lotus pond where there are always lots of people coming and going?"

9   The thief was so excited that all he could say was "Yes" and "That's right" until he was able to leave.

> Make a prediction. What do you think happens next?
> _____

10   For many days the thief studied the situation. Then one very dark night, he climbed the palace wall and stole the hand mill from beside the lotus pond.

11   He was brimming with pride and confidence as he made his way back to the wall. But once outside the palace, he was overcome with fear of being discovered. His **heart skipped a beat** every time he met someone on the street. He decided to steal a boat and go to his hometown to hide because he knew that once the theft was discovered, everyone in the city and on the roads would be questioned.

12   Once at sea, the thief lay back in the bow of the boat and laughed. Then he began to sing and dance as he thought about how rich he was going to be. Then he thought about what to request from the hand mill. He did not want to ask for something common and easy to obtain.

> Make a prediction. What do you think happens next?
> _____

13   "Salt! Salt!" he suddenly shouted. "I'll ask for salt! Everyone needs salt. I can sell it and become a rich man. I'll be the richest man in the country."

14   He fell down on his knees and began turning the hand mill, singing as he did, "Salt! Salt! Make some salt!" Then he began dancing and singing about being a rich man.

15   And the hand mill kept turning and turning. Salt spilled over the sides of the small boat but the thief just kept dancing and singing and laughing, all the time thinking about the big house he was going to have and the numerous servants who would serve him **lavish** meals.

Salt appears when the thief asks for it and then turns the hand mill.

> Make a prediction. What do you think happens next?
> _____

16   Finally the boat was so full of salt that it sank to the bottom of the sea. And, since no one has ever told the hand mill to stop, it is still turning and making salt, which is why the sea is salty.

AFTER YOU READ

Check Your Comprehension

A. Circle the letter of the correct response to each question.

1. How would you describe the tone of the story?
   a. light and casual
   b. angry and annoyed
   c. scientific and serious

2. What is the purpose of the story?
   a. to teach a lesson in an entertaining way
   b. to persuade readers to take action
   c. to describe a magical hand mill

B. Number the sentences so that they tell the story in the correct order.

___ The thief climbed the palace wall and stole the hand mill.

___ The thief stole a boat to go to his hometown and hide.

___ A thief heard of a magical hand mill and decided to steal it.

___ The boat sank to the bottom of the sea because it was so heavy with salt.

___ The thief visited a court official and discovered where the hand mill was kept.

___ The thief decided to ask the mill to make salt so that he could sell it and become rich.

Check Your Predictions

C. Compare predictions with a partner. How accurate were your predictions?

D. Complete each of the sentences that follow with the best word or phrase from the box. Be sure to use the correct form of the word or phrase.

make up (one's) mind	(my) heart skipped a beat	chatted
come up with (something)	get something out of (one's) mind	lavish
palace	pond	ministers

1. We went to a fancy restaurant for our anniversary and were served a _____ meal.

2. The prime minister met with his _____ to discuss the new policy.

3. There are beautiful fish swimming in the _____.

4. Do you have any ideas for a topic? I can't _____ one.

5. You need to _____ about where you want to go on your vacation.

6. We took a tour of the _____ where the kings and queens used to live.

7. My friend and I _____ about our boyfriends on the phone last night.

8. I love that song, but now I can't _____.

9. My _____ when I saw that the thief had a knife.

Evaluate Your Ideas

1. Now that you have read the article, reread the statements in the Evaluate the Statements chart on page 164 and mark Agree or Disagree for each one under the After You Read column.

2. Talk with a partner about why any of your new responses differed from the ones you made before you read the article.

3. Find and discuss the specific information in the article that supports each of your opinions.

Sum It Up

Write a one-paragraph summary of "Why the Sea Is Salty." Remember to include only main events from the story in your summary.

_____

_____

_____

_____

Share Your Thoughts

A. Work with a small group. Discuss these questions.

1. What lesson do you think this folktale is trying to teach?
2. Do you think the story is entertaining? Why or why not?
3. What is your favorite part of the story? Why?
4. If you owned the magic hand mill, what would you ask for?

B. Choose one of the questions in Exercise A and write a paragraph about it.

_____

_____

_____

_____

_____

_____

READING 2: Why Is the Ocean Salty?

BEFORE YOU READ

Many folktales try to explain natural phenomena in the world. You have just read a folktale that offers a lighthearted explanation for why the ocean is salty. Now you are going to read a more serious and scientific explanation.

Activate Your Background Knowledge

A. Discuss these questions in small groups.

1. What are the differences between swimming in the ocean and swimming in a lake or river?

2. Have you ever wondered why the ocean is salty? Do you have any ideas about how salt gets into the ocean?

Preview and Predict

B. Read the title and headings of the article on pages 173–174. Look at the chart and photo and read the captions. Can you guess what the article will be about? Think of several topics that might be discussed in the article.

1. _____

2. _____

3. _____

4. _____

Preview the Vocabulary

C. The words and phrases in the box are boldfaced in the article. Use context clues to guess the meaning of the boldfaced words in the exercise. Then compare answers with a partner.

Words to Watch

cycle	evaporate	hydrothermal vent
release	salinity	outlets
desalinate	alter	extract

1. But how does the salt get from the rocks and soil into the oceans? It's all part of a **cycle** of related events that happen again and again in the same order.

_____

2. The heat from the sun causes some of the ocean water to **evaporate** (go from a liquid to a gas), but the salt is left behind in the ocean.

_____

(continued)

3. As volcanoes erupt on the ocean floor, heat from the volcanic eruption causes minerals to dissolve, and salts are **released** into the water.

_____

4. A **hydrothermal vent** is an opening in the seafloor from which hot, salty water flows into the ocean.

_____

5. Scientists have determined that the level of the ocean's **salinity**, or amount of salt in the water, has stayed the same for millions or perhaps even a billion years.

_____

6. The main reason is that lakes have **outlets**, rivers and streams carrying water away from lakes.

_____

7. Still, scientists continue to experiment with ways to **desalinate**, or remove salt from water.

_____

8. The ocean has remained salty for millions of years as minerals are released into its water, and it is a difficult challenge to **alter** this process.

_____

9. **Extracting**, or removing, salt from water on a large scale is possible but difficult.

_____

Set a Purpose

You are going to read an article about why the ocean is salty. Write several questions you would like the article to answer.

_____

_____

As you read "Why Is the Ocean Salty?" think about the author's purpose in writing the article.

Why Is the Ocean Salty?
Where Does the Salt Come From?

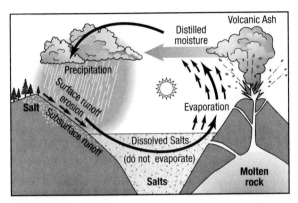

Rivers carry salt to the oceans. Then, as the sun evaporates water from the ocean's surface, the salt is left behind. The evaporated water returns to the Earth as rain.

1   Oceans cover about 70 percent of the surface of the Earth and the water in the oceans is about 3.5 percent salt. That's a lot of salt. In fact, if the oceans dried up completely, there would be enough salt left behind to build a 180-mile-tall, one-mile-thick wall around the equator! Salt is a mineral that is found in soil and rocks. But how does salt get from rocks and soil into the oceans? It's all part of a **cycle** of related events that happen again and again in the same order. As rain falls, water flows over the land and through rivers. On its way, it picks up small amounts of mineral salts from the rocks and soil of the riverbeds. Rivers then carry the salty water to the ocean. Scientists estimate that about four billion tons of salt are carried to the oceans annually. What happens next? The heat from the sun causes some of the ocean water to **evaporate** (go from a liquid to a gas), but the salt is left behind in the ocean. The evaporated water returns to the Earth as

rain, and the cycle starts all over again. Since this has been going on for millions of years, the oceans now have a lot of salt.

What Are Other Sources of Salt?

2   In addition to salt brought in by rivers, there are other sources of salt in the ocean. One is underwater volcanoes. As volcanoes erupt on the ocean floor, heat from the volcanic eruption causes minerals to dissolve, and salts are **released** into the water. Another continual source of salt is hydrothermal vents in the ocean floor. A **hydrothermal vent** is an opening in the seafloor from which hot, salty water flows into the ocean. You can think of a hydrothermal vent as a chimney in the ocean floor.

One source of salt is hydrothermal vents on the ocean floor.

Why Doesn't the Ocean Get Saltier?

3   If salt is constantly being added to ocean water, one might wonder why the salt level stays the same. Why doesn't the ocean get

(continued)

saltier as more salt is released into seawater over the years? Scientists have determined that the level of the ocean's **salinity,** or amount of salt in the water, has stayed the same for millions or perhaps even a billion years. They have observed that approximately the same amount of salt that rivers and hydrothermal processes put into the ocean water is constantly being removed from the water. In other words, the salt gets used up. For one thing, some of the salt is used by organisms. Clams, for example, remove salts from the water to make their shells. In addition, if more water is removed from the oceans through evaporation than is replaced by river water flowing in, salt starts to settle on the ocean floor. Therefore, the level of salt in ocean water remains fairly constant.

Why Isn't Lake Water Salty?

4   Some people prefer swimming in oceans, while others prefer going to lakes to swim. One obvious difference in the water in the two locations is the degree of salt. Why is it that the oceans are so salty, whereas lakes have a relatively low salt content? The main reason is that lakes have **outlets,** rivers and streams carrying water away from lakes. Water flows in and out of lakes, so the lake water has a lower concentration of salt. Exceptions are the Great Salt Lake in Utah and the Dead Sea in the Middle East. In these lakes, there are no outlets; rivers carry water into the lakes but not out. As water evaporates into the air, the salt is left in these lakes.

How Can We Use Ocean Water?

5   Almost three-quarters of the earth's surface is covered with water. The vast oceans of the world would seem to be an almost limitless supply of water for the world's population. However, the presence of salt makes this water unusable for many purposes, such as irrigation or human consumption. Still, scientists continue to experiment with ways to **desalinate,** or remove salt from, water. There has been some remarkable success, especially in Middle Eastern countries such as Saudi Arabia. Up to now, however, desalination methods have proved to be quite expensive. The ocean has remained salty for millions of years as minerals are released into its water, and it is a difficult challenge to **alter** this process. **Extracting,** or removing, salt from water on a large scale is possible but difficult. It requires first filtering the ocean water to remove salt and then treating it with chemicals at high pressure. It's a process that is both costly and time-consuming.

AFTER YOU READ

Check Your Comprehension

A.   Circle the letter of the answer that correctly completes each statement or answers the question.

1. The article mainly describes _____.
   a. the difference between lakes and oceans
   b. why the world's oceans are salty
   c. how to extract salt from the ocean

2. The author explains _____ main cause(s) for the saltiness of the ocean.
   a. one
   b. two
   c. three

3. The author mentions a 180-mile-tall, 1-mile-thick wall around the equator to _____.
   a. create an image of how much salt there is in the oceans
   b. explain how salt is dissolved from rocks
   c. make the reader laugh

4. Underwater volcanoes and hydrothermal vents _____.
   a. add salt to the ocean from openings in the seafloor
   b. remove salt from the ocean floor
   c. have nothing to do with salt in the ocean

5. According to the author, desalination methods are _____.
   a. simple and cost-effective
   b. difficult and expensive
   c. successful everywhere

6. Lakes have a lower salt content than oceans because _____.
   a. there are fewer oceans than lakes
   b. lakes have outlets that carry water away
   c. lake water evaporates into the air

7. The word vast in paragraph 5 means _____.
   a. huge
   b. salty
   c. wet

8. The purpose of this article is to _____.
   a. entertain
   b. persuade
   c. inform

9. The author's tone can be described as _____.
   a. straightforward
   b. hesitant
   c. playful

10. What is the main pattern of organization used in this article?
    a. comparison and contrast
    b. cause/effect
    c. enumeration

Pronoun Reference

B. Read the following sentences from the article. Notice each underlined pronoun and look for the noun it refers to. Write the noun on the line.

1. In addition to salt carried in by rivers, there are other sources of salt in the ocean. <u>One</u> is underwater volcanoes.

   One = _____

2. The water dissolves salt out of the rocks and carries the salt into rivers, which then carry <u>it</u> to the ocean.

   it = _____

3. Scientists have determined that the level of the ocean's salinity, or amount of salt in the water, has stayed the same for millions or perhaps even a billion years. <u>They</u> have observed that about the same amount of salt that rivers and hydrothermal processes put into the ocean water is constantly being removed from the water.

   They = _____

4. Some people prefer swimming in oceans, while <u>others</u> prefer going to lakes to swim.

   others = _____

5. Extracting salt from water on a large scale requires first filtering the ocean water and then treating <u>it</u> with chemicals at high pressure.

   it = _____

Sharpen Your Vocabulary Skills

CONNOTATION AND DENOTATION

The denotation of a word is the dictionary definition of the word. The connotation is the emotion or idea that the word makes you think of, but the connotation is not part of the actual meaning. It is the **idea** that is often associated with the word.

When you saw the word "king" in Reading 1, you probably knew the meaning of the word. A king is a man who is ruler of a country because he is from the royal family. However, when you hear the word "king," what ideas come to your mind? These ideas are connotations. Make a list of connotations of the word "king."

powerful, _____

_____

Write the connotation that each of these words has for you. Then compare ideas with a partner.

Word	Connotation	Denotation
gold		
magic		
thief		
scholar		
minister		
palace		
night		
city		
hometown		
servant		

LEARNING MORE COLLOCATIONS

In Chapter 7 you learned about collocations, or words that go together. Here are some more examples of verb + noun collocations from the folktale "Why the Sea Is Salty."

Verb + Noun Collocations

come up with a plan
sparked his interest
overcome with fear
was brimming with pride

Use the words and phrases in the box to complete the collocations that follow.

brim with	overcome with	sparked	come up with

1. _____ her imagination
2. _____ an idea
3. _____ confidence
4. _____ joy
5. _____ a solution
6. _____ an outcry
7. _____ tears
8. _____ fear
9. _____ a revolution
10. _____ a topic
11. _____ curiosity

Noun + verb collocations are also common in English. Look at the noun + verb collocations from the article "Why Is the Ocean Salty?"

Noun + Verb Collocations

volcanoes erupt
rain falls
water flows

Here are some more related noun + verb collocations you should learn.

snow falls/melts	water freezes	grass grows
wind blows	lightening strikes	earth rotates
ice melts	hurricanes/storms hit	stars twinkle/shine
temperatures rise/fall/drop	flowers bloom/wilt	sun shines/rises/sets

Explore the Web

Use the Internet to find answers to these questions.

1. What are the four major oceans on earth?

2. Some experts feel that there is a fifth ocean. What is it called?

3. What is the largest ocean in the world? How deep is it in feet? In meters?

4. Which ocean is slowly getting smaller?

5. Which ocean is slowly getting larger?

6. How much higher is sea level today than it was 2,500 years ago?

7. How many species of organisms do scientists estimate there are in the ocean?

8. Ocean sponges are being tested to help fight what disease?

Go Beyond the Text

Work in a group of three or four classmates. Choose a folktale you know, or make up a folktale. Discuss the characters in the story and make a list of the events in the folktale. Choose one person in the group to tell the folktale to your classmates or act it out with the people in your group.